Traeger Grill Cookbook

The complete Guide with 60+ Irresistible and Flavorful

Recipes from Classic to Adventurous

BBQ Pitmaster

Legal & Disclaimer

The information contained in this book and its contents is not designed to replace or take the place of any form of medical or professional advice; and is not meant to replace the need for independent medical, financial, legal or other professional advice or services, as may be required. The content and information in this book have been provided for educational and entertainment purposes only.

The content and information contained in this book have been compiled from sources deemed reliable, and it is accurate to the best of the Author's knowledge, information, and belief. However, the author cannot guarantee its accuracy and validity and cannot be held liable for any errors and/or omissions. Further, changes are periodically made to this book as and when needed. Where appropriate and/or necessary, you must consult a professional (including but not limited to your doctor, attorney, financial advisor or such other professional advisor) before using any of the suggested remedies, techniques, or information in this book.

Upon using the contents and information contained in this book, you agree to hold harmless the Author from and against any damages, costs, and expenses, including any legal fees potentially resulting from the application of any of the information provided by this book. This disclaimer applies to any loss, damages or injury caused by the use and application, whether directly or indirectly, of any advice or information presented, whether for breach of contract, tort, negligence, personal injury, criminal intent, or under any other cause of action.

You agree to accept all risks of using the information presented inside this book.

You agree that by continuing to read this book, where appropriate and/or necessary, you shall consult a professional (including but not limited to your doctor, attorney,

or financial advisor or such other advisor as needed) before using any of the suggested remedies, techniques, or information in this book.

Table of Contents

INTRODUCTION

Today, barbecue is everywhere, from airport terminals around the globe to cosmopolitan cities where it was once thought impossible to find true, down-southern home cooking—hey, don't laugh, these days even New York City has a real barbecue. But wherever you find yourself enjoying some tender, juicy meat, all roads lead back to Texas, the Carolinas, Memphis, and Kansas City—the four points of the barbecue compass.

With the rise in popularity of barbecue, what defines real barbecue is easy to overlook. After all, people use the term casually in everyday conversation. "Come over; we're having a barbecue on the Fourth of July!" The thing is: If for a hot second you throw burgers, steaks, and hot dogs on a grill, that's not true barbecue, that's grilling. 'Real barbecue' takes time, perseverance, and preparation. Through a transformative cooking process, real barbecue is about sending hard, fatty cuts of meat, an effort rewarded with tender morsels that melt in your mouth. Real barbecue—flavored with hardwoods such as apple, hickory, and oak trees—is about smoking. And that is the way it ought to be. So if you're ready to move on from the grill to real barbecue, this is the book for you.

When making real Southern barbecue, what is the key ingredient? If you guess that it is smoking, you're right. Smokers come in all forms and sizes these days, and they run on all kinds of power sources, including natural gas, propane, charcoal, and even electricity. But the one thing that they all have in common is that to produce the smoke that both cooks and flavors the meat, they have to burn wood in some way.

How Smoking Works

Originally, barbecue involved digging a pit in the dirt, making a wood fire, and letting embers burn down. The meat was then slow-cooked over the embers in a spit and smoked in the process. A steel log pit whose exclusive fuel source is wood is the modern-day version of such a setup. And the formula remains the same even if your system isn't quite as fancy—smoke combined with low, indirect heat and plenty of time.

Smokers kick things up a couple of notches. The advantages of putting the meat in an enclosed appliance over cooking it in an open pit are as follows: By trapping the flame, it shortens the cooking time, and by trapping and spreading the smoke, it imparts greater flavor. Today, the way

Benefits of a Traeger Pellet Grill

RETAINS AND ENHANCES TASTE
The wood pellet based grills are well appreciated by the users since the wood pellets burnt with control, cooks the meats while retaining the juiciness.

VERSATILE COOKING
Its versatility comes from the control over the temperature offered in this amazing grill range.

IGNITE, SET AND FORGET
Fill the pellets, ignite the fire, set the temperature, lay your recipe on the grill and enjoy what you were doing.

WIDESPREAD AND GROWING COMMUNITY
A huge count of its die hard customers share major solutions to the minor issues, recipes and of course joy of eating fresh and delicious smoky food.

smokers operate is pretty easy. The source of smoke and heat are separated, and smoke is produced using wood. In the case of wood-burning pits, the fuel is also wood. But wood is usually applied directly to the fuel or indirectly exposed to heat, allowing it to smolder. Adjustable vents (and chimneys, depending on the design) provide a way to control the temperature and smoke density and enable the circulation and escape of smoke.

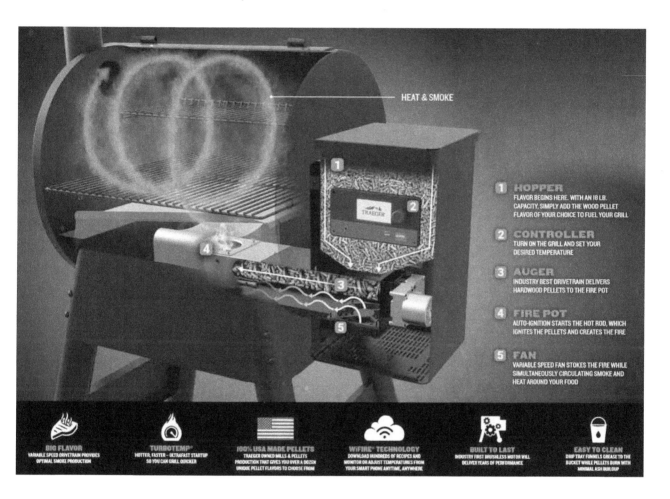

HEAT & SMOKE

1 HOPPER
FLAVOR BEGINS HERE. WITH AN 18 LB. CAPACITY, SIMPLY ADD THE WOOD PELLET FLAVOR OF YOUR CHOICE TO FUEL YOUR GRILL

2 CONTROLLER
TURN ON THE GRILL AND SET YOUR DESIRED TEMPERATURE

3 AUGER
INDUSTRY BEST DRIVETRAIN DELIVERS HARDWOOD PELLETS TO THE FIRE POT

4 FIRE POT
AUTO-IGNITION STARTS THE HOT ROD, WHICH IGNITES THE PELLETS AND CREATES THE FIRE

5 FAN
VARIABLE SPEED FAN STOKES THE FIRE WHILE SIMULTANEOUSLY CIRCULATING SMOKE AND HEAT AROUND YOUR FOOD

BIG FLAVOR
VARIABLE SPEED DRIVETRAIN PROVIDES OPTIMAL SMOKE PRODUCTION

TURBOTEMP
HOTTER, FASTER – ULTRAFAST STARTUP SO YOU CAN GRILL QUICKER

100% USA MADE PELLETS
TRAEGER OWNED MILLS & PELLETS PRODUCTION THAT GIVES YOU OVER A DOZEN UNIQUE PELLET FLAVORS TO CHOOSE FROM

WiFIRE TECHNOLOGY
DOWNLOAD HUNDREDS OF RECIPES AND MONITOR OR ADJUST TEMPERATURES FROM YOUR SMART PHONE ANYTIME, ANYWHERE

BUILT TO LAST
INDUSTRY FIRST BRUSHLESS MOTOR WILL DELIVER YEARS OF PERFORMANCE

EASY TO CLEAN
DRIP TRAY FUNNELS GREASE TO THE BUCKET WHILE PELLETS BURN WITH MINIMAL ASH BUILDUP

CHAPTER 1: POULTRY RECIPES

1. Chicken Sliders Barbecue with Simple Slaw

Ingredients:

- 4 rolls slider, split
- 1 breast smoked chicken, thinly sliced
- 1 cup simple coleslaw
- 1/4 cup Kansas City-style barbecue sauce

Directions:

1. Place 1/4 of the sliced chicken on the heel of every bun and top with coleslaw.
2. Drizzle over the coleslaw with the barbecue sauce, and top with the bun's crown.
3. Serve the sliders with some classic potato salad to turn this into a complete meal.

2. Chicken-Tortilla Kicked-Up Soup

Ingredients:

- 1 tbsp. cumin
- 3 tbsp. vegetable oil
- 1 chopped yellow onion
- 3 carrots, chopped
- 3 celery stalks, chopped, leaves reserved if the kosher salt is bright green
- 1 tsp. powdered ancho chili
- 1 tsp. chipotle chili powder
- 1 tsp. chili powder Guajillo®
- 4 cups chicken broth
- 1 cup canned tomatoes, diced
- 1 chicken carcass, smoked
- 1/2 smoked chicken, meat removed from the bone, chopped
- 3 maize tortillas, cut into strips

Directions:

1. Heat the cumin seeds in the oil in a large saucepan over medium heat for 3 to 4 minutes, or until fragrant.
2. Add the onion, carrots, and celery and raise the heat to medium-high. Cook for six to seven minutes, or until slightly tender.
3. Add the ancho chili powder, the chipotle chili powder, the chili powder Guajillo®, the chicken broth, the onions, the celery leaves (if they are used), and the chicken carcass (if they are used).
4. Bring to a simmer and cook until the vegetables are tender, or for around 15 to 20 minutes.

5. To allow the flavors to meld, add the chopped meat and simmer for 3 to 4 minutes.

6. Attach the tortilla strips and simmer for around 1 minute, or until tender.

7. Divide it into 8 bowls and serve immediately.

3. Glazed Chicken Quarters

Ingredients:

- 6 chicken quarters
- 1/3 cup dry rub
- 1 cup mild barbecue sauce
- 2 tbsp. vegetable oil, or more, for brushing the grate

Directions:

1. For 15 to 30 minutes, soak 4 1/2 cups of wood chips in water.
2. Clean and pat the chicken dry and let it hit room temperature.
3. Preheat the smoker to 225°F or 250°F, and, following the directions of the maker, add the wood chips.
4. Roll up a clean, lint-free kitchen towel and drop it in some vegetable oil. If the grates have not been oiled, grab the towel and smooth it over the grates using tongs.
5. Thoroughly coat the chicken with the dry rub and put in a single layer on the grates.
6. For 2 1/4 to 2 3/4 hours, close the cooking compartment and smoke. Soak and replenish additional wood chips as needed—add more wood if you no longer see smoke escaping from the chimneys or vents.
7. Remove the chicken from the smoker. Heat 2 tablespoons of vegetable oil in a large frying pan over high heat. When the oil is hot, brown the chicken for 1 1/2 to 2 minutes on each side or until the skin is crisp.
8. Brush the barbecue sauce over the chicken and return the chicken to the smoker for 15 to 20 minutes, or until at least 160°F is read by an instant-read thermometer inserted into the meat without touching the bone. Prior to serving, let the chicken rest for 5 minutes.

4. Chicken Grilled with Chipotle Sauce

Ingredients:

- 2 tbsp. lard or neutral oil, such as maize or canola, for brushing chicken, or more
- 1 medium-size white onion, chopped
- 2 chipotle chilies, canned, to taste
- 2 cups chopped and cored tomatoes
- Salt and pepper, to taste, pepper
- 8 chicken thighs, drumsticks, or whole legs
- 2 garlic cloves, cut in half
- Fresh cilantro, cut
- Garnish leaves
- Garnish lime wedges

Directions:

1. Light charcoal, wood fire, or preheat a gas grill—the fire should be moderately hot, the grill portion should be cooler than the rest, and the heat source rack should be 4 to 6 inches.
2. In a medium saucepan or skillet, add lard or oil and turn the heat to medium. When it is hot, add the onion and cook for 5 to 10 minutes, occasionally stirring, until browned. Combine the chilies, onions, and 1/2 cup of sugar.
3. Change the heat so that the mixture simmers constantly, but not violently. Cook for 15 minutes or so, stirring regularly until the chilies and tomatoes are tender. When required, taste and add salt and pepper.
4. Cool for a few minutes until the chipotle sauce is ready, then cut the chipotle stems, place the mixture in a blender, and purée—it is possible to make the sauce a few days in advance.

Meanwhile, rub the chicken with the garlic cloves on the cut side, brush with the oil, and season with salt and pepper to taste.

5. Put the chicken skin-side up on the least hot spot of the grill.

6. Turn the chicken over when the fat has returned a little.

7. Move the chicken to the hottest part of the grill after 20 minutes or so.

8. Brush it on both sides with chipotle sauce when the chicken is just about cooked, and cook for just another minute or two.

9. Garnish with lime wedges and cilantro, and then serve.

5. Chicken Grilled with Mediterranean Flavors

Ingredients:

- Salt and black pepper freshly ground
- 1 tsp. thyme-fresh leaves
- 1 tsp. fresh rosemary leaves, chopped
- 1/2 tsp. fresh lavender leaves, chopped, optional
- 1⁄4 cup chopped fresh parsley
- As needed, extra virgin olive oil
- 8 chicken thighs, drumsticks, or a combination thereof
- 8 leaves of bay
- 2 lemons, cut into quarts

Directions:

1. Start a fire with charcoal, wood, or heat a gas grill. The fire should only be moderately hot, the grill portion should be kept cooler than the rest, and the rack should be 4 to 6 inches from the source of the heat.
2. Combine the salt, pepper, thyme, rosemary, lavender, and parsley in a small cup. To make a paste, add enough olive oil to it. Loosen the chicken skin and slip the bay leaf between the skin and the meat, then apply a portion of the herb mixture. Sprinkle with salt and pepper and press the skin back onto the meat.
3. Put the chicken skin-side up on the least hot spot of the grill. Turn the chicken over when the fat has returned a little. Move the chicken to the hottest part of the grill after 20 minutes or so, brush it with a little olive oil, and cook until the meat is finished and the skin is well browned. Serve with wedges of lemon.

6. Mock Tandoori Chicken Twice-Cooked

Ingredients:

- 8 chicken thighs
- 2 spoonfuls peanut or vegetable oil
- 1 onion, medium-sized, chopped
- Salt and black pepper, freshly ground
- 4 or 5 garlic cloves, crushed, peeled
- 1 (2-inch piece) fresh ginger, peeled, chopped, or 2 tsp. dried ginger
- 1 tbsp. cilantro, ground
- 1 tsp. cardamom, ground
- 1 spoon paprika
- 1 tsp. cumin field
- Fresh chilies or red pepper flakes to taste, or cayenne, optional
- 3 cups plain yogurt

Directions:

1. Preheat the oven to 300°F. Place the chicken in a deep pan to roast.
2. Pour oil into a large skillet over medium-high heat.
3. Add the onion, sprinkle with salt and pepper, and cook for about 2 minutes, occasionally stirring, until it softens and starts to color.
4. Add garlic and ginger and cook and stir for an additional 2 minutes.
5. Stir in the ground spices, and cook for no more than a minute or until only fragrant.
6. Stir in the yogurt, then cover the chicken with the mixture.
7. Cover and put it in the oven and bake for around 1 1/2 hours until the chicken is cooked through.

8. You can make chicken a few days in advance, or if you're not going to grill right away, place the whole pan in the fridge after it's cooled down a bit.

9. Light a grill with charcoal or gas—the rack should be about 4 inches away from the source of flame.

10. Remove the chicken from the yogurt sauce and scrape the excess away.

11. Grill over direct heat until the skin is crisp and crispy and the meat dries out a bit, rotating once or twice for around 15 minutes.

12. Serve at room temperature or hotter.

7. Cambodia Barbecued Chicken

Ingredients:

- 6 chicken wings, thighs, and drumsticks, separated
- 1 tsp. Kosher salt
- ½ tsp. freshly ground pepper
- ½ cup barbecue paste lemongrass, recipe follows

Directions:

1. Place the chicken on a baking sheet and season with salt and pepper. Slice the barbecue paste log into disks and dot it with chicken.
2. When the charcoal is hot, place the chicken on the grill, with its pasted side facing up. Depending on your grill, cover and cook for 20 to 30 minutes or until the juices run free. Don't take turns. Scrape the paste off the chicken carefully and discard it. Serve with rice.

8. Barbecue Lemongrass Paste

Ingredients:

- 2 fresh lemongrass stalks
- 1 (1-inch) piece fresh turmeric, frozen, see note
- 1 (1-inch) piece frozen galangal, see note
- 1 shallot, peeled
- 1 fresh lemon leaf, frozen, see note
- 1 garlic clove, peeled
- 2 tbsp. cold butter

Directions:

1. In a food processor, pulverize lemongrass.
2. With the exception of butter, add the remaining ingredients and refine them into a fine paste.
3. To ensure that the mash is good enough, take a tiny sample. It's going to taste bad. If there are any fibrous bits left, process them until they are gone.
4. Add butter and process the ingredients are blended together.
5. Remove the paste from the bowl and shape it into a 1-inch diameter log. Put the log in plastic wrap place it in the freezer.

Note: Before grilling, broiling, or baking, this paste can be used to enliven chicken, veal, or fish like tuna, swordfish, or Chilean sea bass. It has to be in the freezer for approximately a month.

Note: In Asian markets, turmeric, galangal, and lemon leaf are available.

9. Grilled Tabasco Chicken

Ingredients:

- 6 (3 1/2 lb.) chicken legs, approx.
- 1 tbsp. soy sauce
- 1 tbsp. ketchup
- 1 tbsp. vinegar with cider
- 1 tbsp. Tabasco® sauce

Directions:

1. Trim off the drumstick tips and cut halfway through the joint, linking each leg's thigh and drumstick.
2. In a tray, mix the soy sauce, ketchup, vinegar, and Tabasco® sauce, and roll the chicken legs in the marinade.
3. Place the legs on the side of the skin on the rack of a hot grill about 10 inches from the fire and cook for about 10 minutes. Turn the legs over and cook on the other side for about 10 minutes. Switch them again and cook them on the side of the skin for 10 more minutes.
4. Remove the legs from the heat to cool before serving for 5 minutes.

10. Hot Smoked Wings

Ingredients:

- 2 lb. chicken wings or drumettes
- Vegetable oil, used to brush grates
- 2 tbsp. "hot n tangy" dry rub
- 1 cup Buffalo® sauce

Directions:

1. For 15 to 30 minutes, soak 3 cups of wood chips in water.
2. Clean and pat the chicken dry and let hit room temperature.
3. Preheat the smoker to 225°F or 250°F, and, following the directions of the maker, add the wood chips.
4. Roll up a clean, lint-free kitchen towel and drop it in some vegetable oil. If the grates have not been oiled, grab the towel and smooth it over the grates using tongs.
5. Thoroughly coat the chicken with the dry rub, and put it in a single layer on the grates.
6. Close the cooking compartment and smoke for 2 to 2 1/2 hours, or until at least 160°F is read by an instant-read thermometer inserted into the meat without touching the bone. Soak and replenish additional wood chips as needed—add more wood if you no longer see smoke escaping from the chimneys or vents.
7. Place the wings and the sauce into a large bowl and toss them together.

11. Smoked Chicken Drumsticks

Ingredients:

- 2 lb. drumsticks for chicken
- 2 tbsp. dry rub
- 2 tbsp. vegetable oil, or more, for brushing the grates

Directions:

1. For 15 to 30 minutes, soak 4 1/2 cups of wood chips in water.
2. Clean and pat the chicken dry and let it hit room temperature.
3. Preheat the smoker to 225°F or 250°F, and, following the directions of the maker, add the wood chips.
4. Roll up a clean, lint-free kitchen towel and drop it in some vegetable oil. If the grates have not been oiled, grab the towel and smooth it over the grates using tongs.
5. Thoroughly coat the chicken with the dry rub and put in a single layer on the grates.
6. Close the cooking compartment and smoke for 2 1/2 to 3 hours, or until at least 160°F is read by an instant-read thermometer inserted into the meat without touching the bone. Soak and replenish additional wood chips as needed—add more wood if you no longer see smoke escaping from the chimneys or vents.
7. Pour 2 tablespoons of vegetables into a large saucepan and place over high heat. Add the drumsticks when the oil is hot, and brown it all over for 3 to 5 minutes, or until the skin is crisp. Prior to serving, let the drumsticks rest for 5 minutes.
8. Try serving this with the Sweet Home Alabama® barbecue sauce.

12. Bacon-Wrapped Chicken Breasts

Ingredients:

- 6 chicken breasts, boneless, skinless
- 8 cups brine all-purpose
- 1 lb. vegetable oil, or bacon, for brushing the grates

Directions:

1. Submerge the chicken in the brine for 1 to 1 1/2 hours in a non-reactive container.
2. For 15 to 30 minutes, soak 3 cups of wood chips in water.
3. Dry the chicken, pat it and let it hit room temperature.
4. Preheat the smoker to 225°F or 250°F, and, following the directions of the maker, add the wood chips.
5. Roll up a clean, lint-free kitchen towel and drop it in some vegetable oil. If the grates have not been oiled, grab the towel and smooth it over the grates using tongs. With the bacon, cover the breasts and put them on the grates in a single sheet.
6. Close the cooking compartment and smoke for 2 to 2 1/2 hours or until at least 160°F is read by an instant-read thermometer inserted into the meat. Soak and replenish additional wood chips as needed—add more wood if you no longer see smoke escaping from the chimneys or vents.
7. Prior to serving, let the chicken rest for 5 minutes.

13. Smoky Spicy Chicken Thighs

Ingredients:

- 2 lb. chicken thighs, bone-in, skin-on
- 2 tsp. dry rub Texas®
- 2 tbsp. vegetable oil, or more, for brushing the grate

Directions:

1. For 15 to 30 minutes, soak 4 1/2 cups of wood chips in water.
2. Clean and pat the chicken dry and let it hit room temperature.
3. Preheat the smoker to 225°F or 250°F, and, following the directions of the maker, add the wood chips.
4. Roll up a clean, lint-free kitchen towel and drop it in some vegetable oil. If the grates have not been oiled, grab the towel and smooth it over the grates using tongs.
5. Thoroughly coat the chicken with the dry rub and put in a single layer on the grates.
6. Close the cooking compartment and smoke for 2 1/2 to 3 hours, or until at least 160°F is read by an instant-read thermometer inserted into the meat without touching the bone. Soak and replenish additional wood chips as needed—add more wood if you no longer see smoke from escaping the chimneys or vents.
7. Heat 2 tablespoons of vegetable oil in a large frying pan over high heat. Add the thighs and brown them skin-side down for 1 1/2 to 2 minutes or until the skin is crisp when the oil is hot. Until serving, rest for 5 minutes.

   Smoking Tip: Soaking wood chips prevents them from burning up instantly, particularly on charcoal, when you add them to the firebox.

14. Barbecue Chicken Salad with Dressing of Buttermilk

Ingredients:

- 2 bacon strips
- 8 cups mixed greens, such as frisée, radicchio, and endive
- 1⁄2 fennel bulb, cored and sliced thinly
- 3 tbsp. buttermilk dressing
- 1 chicken breast, smoked, sliced
- 2 tbsp. Kansas City-style barbecue sauce

Directions:

1. Cook the bacon in a saucepan over high heat for 1 1⁄2 to 2 minutes, or until crisp on one's hands.
2. Bring the heat to low, turn the bacon and cook for 1 to 2 minutes on the other side.
3. Remove the bacon and set aside.
4. With the buttermilk dressing, throw the mixed greens and fennel bulb in a wide bowl, and crumble the bacon on top.
5. Divide and top with the chicken between 2 plates. Drizzle the chicken with (if using) barbecue sauce and serve immediately.
6. Serve with a grilled corn side "on the cob" with herb butter for a more substantial meal.

15. Smoked Turkey Legs

Ingredients:

- 6 turkey legs
- 1 gal apple juice
- 1/2 cup dry rub
- 2 tbsp. vegetable oil, or more, brushing the grates

Directions:

1. Submerge the turkey in the brine in a non-reactive tub for 3 to 4 hours.
2. For 15 to 30 minutes, soak 6 cups of wood chips in water.
3. Dry the turkey and let it hit room temperature.
4. Preheat the smoker to 225°F or 250°F, and, following the directions of the maker, add the wood chips.
5. Roll up a clean, lint-free kitchen towel and drop it in some vegetable oil. If the grates have not been oiled, grab the towel and smooth it over the grates using tongs.
6. Thoroughly coat the legs in the dry rub and put them in a single layer on the grates.
7. Close the cooking compartment and smoke for about 4 hours, or until at least 160°F is read by an instant-read thermometer inserted into the meat without touching the bone. Soak and replenish additional wood chips as needed—add more wood if you no longer see smoke escaping from the chimneys or vents.
8. Heat 2 tablespoons of vegetable oil in a large frying pan over high heat. Add the turkey and brown it on each side for 1 1/2 to 2 minutes when the oil is hot, or until the skin is crisp. Until serving, let the turkey rest for 10 minutes.

16. Smoked Turkey Breasts

Ingredients:

- 1 turkey breast, bone-in, skin-on
- 1 gal citrus brine
- 1/3 cup dry rub
- 2 tbsp. vegetable oil, or more, for brushing the grates

Directions:

1. Submerge the turkey in the brine overnight in a non-reactive tub.
2. For 15 to 30 minutes, soak 9 cups of wood chips in water.
3. Dry the turkey and let it hit room temperature.
4. Preheat the smoker to 225°F or 250°F, and, following the directions of the maker, add the wood chips.
5. Roll up a clean, lint-free kitchen towel and drop it in some vegetable oil. If the grates have not been oiled, grab the towel and smooth it over the grates using tongs.
6. Thoroughly coat the turkey with the dry rub and put it on the grates.
7. Close the cooking compartment and smoke for 4 to 6 hours, or until at least 160°F is read by an instant-read thermometer inserted into the meat without touching the bone. Soak and replenish additional wood chips as needed—add more wood if you no longer see smoke escaping from the chimneys or vents.
8. Heat 2 tablespoons of vegetable oil in a large frying pan over high heat. Add turkey and brown skin-side down for 1 1/2 to 2 minutes or until the skin is crisp and the oil is hot. Before serving, let the turkey rest for 10 minutes.

17. Thanksgiving Smoked Turkey

Ingredients:

- 1 (12-pound) turkey
- 2 gal of brine all-purpose
- 1/2 cup dry rub
- 2 tbsp. vegetable oil, or more, for brushing the grates

Directions:

1. Submerge the turkey in the brine overnight in a non-reactive tub.
2. For 15 to 30 minutes, soak 12 cups of wood chips in water.
3. Dry the turkey and let it hit room temperature.
4. Preheat the smoker to 225°F or 250°F, and, following the directions of the maker, add the wood chips.
5. Roll up a clean, lint-free kitchen towel and drop it in some vegetable oil. If the grates have not been oiled, grab the towel and smooth it over the grates using tongs.
6. Thoroughly coat the turkey with the dry rub and put it on the grates, breast-side up.
7. Close the cooking compartment and smoke for around 6 1/2 hours, or until at least 160°F is read by an instant-read thermometer inserted into the meat without touching the bone. Soak and replenish additional wood chips as needed—add more wood if you no longer see smoke escaping from the chimneys or vents.
8. Heat 2 tablespoons of vegetable oil in a large frying pan over high heat. When the oil is hot, add the turkey and brown each side for 1 1/2 to 2 minutes or until the skin is crisp. Prior to serving, let the turkey rest for 20 minutes.

18. Smoked Chicken Spatchcocked

Ingredients:

- 1 whole chicken
- 1/3 cup dry rub
- 2 tbsp. vegetable oil, or more, for brushing the grates

Directions:

1. For 15 to 30 minutes, soak 4 1/2 cups of wood chips in water.
2. Clean and pat the chicken dry and let it hit room temperature.
3. Preheat the smoker to 225°F or 250°F, and, following the directions of the maker, add the wood chips.
4. Roll up a clean, lint-free kitchen towel and drop it in some vegetable oil. If the grates have not been oiled, grab the towel and smooth it over the grates using tongs.
5. Set the chicken breast-side down on a cutting board. Cut down from both sides of the backbone using kitchen scissors. Split the chicken open and make shallow cuts along the bone that runs down the middle of the breast using a sharp knife. Flip the chicken over and press down on the breast until it breaks, using both hands.
6. Thoroughly coat the chicken with the dry rub and put it on the grates, breast-side up.
7. Close the cooking compartment and smoke for around 2 1/2 to 3 hours, or until at least 160°F is read by an instant-read thermometer inserted into the meat without touching the bone. Soak and replenish additional wood chips as needed—add more wood if you no longer see smoke escaping from the chimneys or vents.
8. Heat 2 tablespoons of vegetable oil in a large frying pan over high heat. Place the chicken, breast side down, and brown it for 1 1/2 to 2 minutes until the is hot, or the skin side is crisp. Before serving, let the chicken rest for 10 minutes.

19. Beer May Chicken

Ingredients:

- 1 chicken whole
- 1/3 cup dry rub
- 1 can American lager, like Budweiser
- 2 tbsp. vegetable oil, or more, for brushing the grates

Directions:

1. For 15 to 30 minutes, soak 3 cups of wood chips in water.
2. Clean and pat the chicken dry and let it hit room temperature.
3. Preheat the smoker to 225°F or 250°F, and, following the directions of the maker, add the wood chips.
4. Roll up a clean, lint-free kitchen towel and drop it in some vegetable oil; if the grates have not been oiled, grab the towel and smooth it over the grates using tongs.
5. Thoroughly coat the chicken with the dry rub and put the beer can in the cavity, right-side up. Place the chicken on the grates, the wings facing up, using the beer can and legs as a three-point stand.
6. Close the cooking compartment and smoke for around 3 to 4 hours, or until at least 160°F is read by an instant-read thermometer inserted into the meat without touching the bone. Soak and replenish additional wood chips as needed—add more wood if you no longer see smoke escaping from the chimneys or vents.
7. Heat 2 tablespoons of vegetable oil in a large frying pan over high heat. When the oil is hot, add the chicken and brown for 1 1/2 to 2 minutes on each side or until the skin is crisp. Until serving, let the chicken rest for 20 minutes.

CHAPTER 2: PORK RECIPES

20. Spareribs Barbecued

Ingredients:

- 1 (1 lb.) can peeled tomatoes or around 1 1⁄4 lb. fresh tomatoes, peeled, chopped
- 1 large onion, finely chopped
- 2 garlic cloves, minced
- 3 tbsp. brown sugar or maple syrup
- 1⁄4 tsp. sauce from Worcestershire
- 1⁄2 cup lemon juice, fresh
- 1 tsp. salt
- Freshly ground pepper, to taste
- Dash Tabasco® sauce
- 1⁄4 tsp. dry mustard
- 1⁄2 tsp. ginger ground
- 1⁄4 tsp. allspice field
- 2 to 3 lb. spareribs

Directions:

1. Mash up the tomatoes inside the can with a tablespoon and dump it into a saucepan. Add all remaining ingredients, bar spareribs, and simmer for about 45 minutes.
2. Pour the sauce over the ribs and set aside in the refrigerator for 2 or 3 hours, and spoon the sauce over the meat at intervals.

3. Place the grill over heat when the charcoal has burnt down and is spread evenly, allowing for 4 to 5 inches (see fire instructions below).

4. Cook the barbeque ribs for at least 1 hour, watching carefully to avoid them from getting burnt. Turn at intervals and carefully apply the marinade so that they spill over the coals as little as possible—do not marinate the meat during the last 5 minutes of grilling and discard the marinade.

21. Spare Ribs for Fatty' Cue

Ingredients:

- 2 cups fish sauce
- 6 garlic cloves, crushed, peeled
- 1 shallot big, sliced
- 1 tbsp. black pepper that is freshly ground
- 1/2 cup sugar granulated
- 2 racks spare pork ribs
- 2 tbsp. Indonesian pepper, toasted and ground, or to taste
- 6 oz. palm sugar
- white toasts, for serving

Directions:

1. In a big pot, mix 1 1/2 cups of fish sauce with garlic, shallot, black pepper, and granulated sugar. At least one gallon of water should be added, then cover and bring to a boil over high heat. Reduce the heat and simmer for 30 minutes. Remove from the heat, position, and chill in a non-reactive container. For at least 6 hours and no longer than 12 hours, drop the ribs in the brine.
2. Lightly remove the ribs from the brine and dust with Indonesian ground pepper.
3. Make a small fire on one side of a grill with a cover, ensuring that all the wood or charcoal is engulfed in flames. Place the ribs on the grill on the side without fire as flames start to die down, leaving flickering coals. At any time, do not let flames hit the meat.
4. Cover the grill vent and cook slightly, check the fire every 30 minutes or so and add a little more fuel if necessary, at about 220°F for about 5 hours, until the meat is separated from the bone and its internal temperature is at least 170°F but not more than 180°F.

5. In the meantime, produce a glaze. In a small pot over a medium flame, mix the palm sugar and 3⁄4 cup of water and heat until the sugar melts. Mix the plain syrup with the remaining half a cup of fish sauce.

6. Glaze heavily and serve when the ribs are ready, with white toasts on the side.

22. Chops of Grilled Pork with Fried Sage Leaves

Ingredients:

- 4 pork loin chops
- 1 lemon (a unit) juice
- 1 garlic clove, minced
- 2 tbsp. olive oil
- Freshly ground pepper and coarse salt to taste
- 1/2 cup vegetable oil, approximately enough for 1/2 inch in a pan
- 30 fresh sage leaves

Directions:

1. Using a combination of lemon juice, garlic, and olive oil to coat the pork chops. At room temperature, marinate for 30 minutes. Season with salt and pepper and barbecue, rotating once for about 20 minutes over hot coals or until cooked through.
2. Heat the vegetable oil and fry the sage leaves for approximately 2 minutes or until crisp. Remove from the heat and place onto paper towels with a slotted spoon, and rinse.
3. Garnish the pork chops with the sage leaves.

23. North Carolina-Pulled Pork style

Ingredients:

- 1 (5 to 6 lb.) pork shoulder, bone-in
- 1/4 cup simple barbecue rub
- 4 cups hickory chips, soaked for 1 hour in cold water and then drained
- For the Vinegar Sauce:
- 1 1/2 cups vinegar, for cider
- 2 tsp. sugar, or to taste
- 1 tbsp. red pepper flakes
- 2 tsp. salt, or to taste
- 1/2 tsp. black pepper, freshly ground

Directions:

1. If using charcoal, preheat the grill to 325°F, generate fire on opposite sides of the grill, or if using gas on one side or opposite sides. Season the rubbed pork.

2. When using charcoal, add fresh coals every hour for the first 4 hours and toss half a cup of wood chips on each mound of coals. Place wood chips in the smoker's box when using gas, and preheat until you see smoke—use all 4 cups at once, depending on the gas grill model, or 1 cup per hour for the first 4 hours.

3. Place pork fat-side up over the drip pan on the grill, away from the fire. Barbecue for 4 to 6 hours, until nicely browned and cooked through, or until the internal temperature is 195°F, so that the meat can be properly shredded afterward.

4. Meanwhile, in a bowl with 3/4 cup of water, combine the ingredients for the vinegar sauce and whisk to blend. If desired, add additional salt or sugar to taste.

5. Move the cooked pork to the cutting board, cover it with foil, and let it rest for about 15 minutes until it is cool enough to treat.

6. Cut the meat and discard any skin, bones, or fat. Cut each piece of pork into shreds about 2 inches long and 1/4-inch wide with fingertips or a fork. Transfer to a metal or foil pan and stir in 1 cup of vinegar sauce, or enough to keep the meat moist and flavorful—or chop the meat finely with a cleaver.

7. Cover with foil to keep warm until served, and put on the grill.

8. Serve in between hamburger buns with the coleslaw and the remaining sauce on the side.

24. Vietnam Pork Kebabs

Ingredients:

- 2 lb. fatty ground pork, shoulder-like
- 3 lemongrass stalks, tender, white and pale green parts only, minced
- 4 shallots, chopped
- 2 garlic cloves, minced
- 1 tbsp. fish sauce
- 2 tsp. sugar
- 1 tsp. turmeric
- 1 tsp. black pepper, ground
- Oil on the grill rack, for brushing
- Whole lettuce leaves,
- Fresh mint
- Cilantro sprigs, for serving
- Nuoc cham, for serving

Directions:

1. In a cup, combine the pork, lemongrass, shallots, garlic, fish sauce, sugar, turmeric, and pepper, and knead the paste very well.
2. Keep a point in one hand with a flat metal skewer (not non-stick, and at least 12 inches long). Dip the other hand in a bowl of water, take a handful of the meat mixture and form it into a small sausage shape with pointed ends around the base of the skewer. Working your way up the skewer, repeat. It should carry 3 or 4 kebabs for each skewer—you can only make 8 patties of meat as well.

3. Lay the finished skewers with fingers on a sheet pan, and smooth kebabs, making sure they are reasonably smooth and stable on skewers. Refrigerate for a minimum of 1 hour.

4. Prepare the barbecue with charcoal, or turn the gas grill to medium-low. On a clean grill rack, spray or brush oil, and set the temperature low. The fire should not be too hot, and the heat source should be at least a few inches from the rack.

5. Gently squeeze kebabs when the rack is hot to make sure they are healthy on skewers and put skewers on the grill. The meat is expected to start gently sizzling—it does not spit and turn black. Cook at least for 7 minutes, until deep brown. Slide a spatula under the kebabs and flip the meat over when it can be readily removed from the grill. Continue to grill until browned and juicy on both sides but also cooked through for a total of 10 to 15 minutes.

6. Wrap a kebab with herbs in a lettuce leaf, then dip in "Nuoc Cham."

25. Pork Loin Grilled with Wine-Salt Rub

Ingredients:

- 2 cups white fruity wine, for example, Riesling or gewürztraminer
- 3/4 tbs. coarse sea salt
- 8 sprigs fresh thyme, leaves stripped, about 2 tbsp. leaves
- 2 strips lemon zest, finely chopped
- 1 tbs. sugar
- 1 (3 1/2 lb.) pork loin, center-cut, boneless, patted dry

Directions:

1. Simmer the wine in a medium, heavy-bottomed saucepan over medium heat until it is hot in 20 to 30 minutes, set the heat to low, and continue to cook.

2. Combine the salt, thyme leaves, lemon zest, and wine reduction in a food processor, and pulse 2 or 3 times. Add sugar and pulse again until the mixture is moist and consistent. Spread it uniformly on a sheet pan if your mixture is moister, and set it out for several hours or overnight on the counter.

3. Put the pork in a pan to roast. Spread about 1/2 cup of salt-wine rub over all the pork—save the remaining rub for another use, keep refrigerated for a month. Cover tightly with plastic wrap and refrigerate overnight or for at least 3 hours.

4. Light the grill for indirect, high-heat cooking, piling on one side of the grill with charcoal and leaving the other side unlit—Turn on the heat only on one side of the grill for gas grills. Spread a piece of foil or put a disposable metal roasting pan on an unlighted side under the grill to catch any drips. Place the pork over the foil on the grill. Cover the grill and cook until the meat hits 140°F in the middle, turning every 1/2 hour, from 1 hour to 1 ½ hour. Place on a cutting board and leave to rest for 10 minutes before carving.

26. Marinated Grilled Pork Loin

Ingredients:

- 1 (1 1/2 lb.) boneless loin roast of rolled pork, tied
- 6 fresh chilies, green, seeded, and finely chopped
- 9 tbsp. peanut oil
- 6 tbsp. lime juice
- 3 tbsp. fresh cilantro, finely minced
- 1 tbsp. garlic, finely minced
- 1 tbsp. sugar

Directions:

1. Place the roast pork in a glass bowl. Mix the remaining ingredients and pour thoroughly over the roasted pork to coat. Cover the bowl and refrigerate for a minimum of 12 hours.
2. Light a charcoal fire 45 minutes before cooking.
3. Remove the pork from the marinade (reserve marinade); when the coals are medium-hot, dry with paper towels and grill, often turning for 10 minutes. Cover the grill with its hood or a makeshift foil lid and roast for 20 minutes, basting often, or until 110°F is read by a thermometer inserted into the thickest part of the loin. (Marinade Discard.)
4. Pull the pork off the grill. Cut into 1-inch-thick slices. Grill slices uncovered, on each side for 4 to 5 minutes, until cooked but still juicy. Immediately serve.

27. Grilled Pork and Peaches

Ingredients:

- 1 (2 lb.) pork butt, boneless, butterflied, trimmed
- 8 to 10 garlic cloves, minced
- 2 tsp. fresh rosemary, minced
- 8 tsp. extra virgin olive oil
- Kosher salt and freshly ground black pepper to taste
- 6 fresh peaches, skin on, cut in half, pitted
- 4 (1/2 stick) tbsp. unsalted butter, sliced into cubes

Directions:

1. Light a fire with a grill in a fire pit, or in a barbecue grill, or set a gas grill on high. Under the sun, position a big, cast-iron pan or double-burner griddle and allow it to get hot. You should let the fire die slightly at this stage with no ill effects. Turn the heat to low while using a gas grill or stove.

2. Meanwhile, place the pork on a work surface and pound to an even thickness of approximately 3/4 inches using a meat mallet.

3. In a small bowl, add the garlic, rosemary, and 6 tablespoons of olive oil together to create a rough paste. Season the pork with salt and pepper vigorously on both sides, then spread 1/2 the garlic mixture on one side and a half on the other side.

4. Brush the pan or griddle with the remaining 2 tablespoons of olive oil, allow it to heat for about 10 minutes or until it shimmers and almost smokes, then put the meat on the hot surface and cook until it forms a nice crust, without touching it.

5. While the meat is cooking, surround it with peaches, cut down on the side, and add butter to the fruit. (Place the peaches in their own oiled pan if you're using two cast-iron skillets.) Let

them cook for around 5 minutes or until they're soft and lightly charred. To keep wet, switch to a dish and tent with foil.

6. Use tongs to turn it over when the meat is well browned on the first side, then cook in the remaining butter for another 5 to 7 minutes. Remove the meat from the carving board and allow it to rest for approximately 5 minutes under the foil tent. Slice the meat and serve the peaches with it.

28. Tenderloin Barbecued Pork

Ingredients:

- 4 garlic cloves, minced
- 2 cups sliced onions
- 1⁄2 cup fresh lemon juice
- 1⁄2 cup sauce for soy
- 1⁄2 cup oil with corn
- 1⁄4 cup sugar
- 3 to 4 tbsp. coriander, ground
- sauce Tabasco®
- 6 (about 3⁄4 lb.) pork tenderloins

Directions:

1. Combine the garlic, onions, lemon juice, soy sauce, oil, sugar, cilantro, and Tabasco sauce in a large bowl, stirring well. (Tabasco sauce, depending on tolerance, should be added to taste—1⁄4 to 1⁄2 teaspoon.)

2. Place whole tenderloins in the marinade, spoon to cover all surfaces, and set aside in the refrigerator for 5 to 6 hours; periodically turn the meat.

3. Set the wire grill above heat when the charcoal has burnt down and is spread evenly, allowing for 4 to 5 inches (see fire instructions above).

4. Stir the marinade and the spoon over the meat, scrape off the bits of vegetables and sauce. Pour the marinade into the cooking pan and simmer while cooking the meat.

5. Lay the tenderloins on the grill, enabling space for turning between parts. Turn the marinade pieces and spoon over the seared surface after about 20 minutes. Repeat to sear each side. Barbeque for 1 hour or more.

6. Spread cooked marinade over each tenderloin upon serving.

29. Buffalo Ribs

Ingredients:

For the rub and ribs:

- 2 tsp. kosher or marine coarse salt
- 2 tsp. lemon pepper
- 2 tsp. powdered garlic
- 2 tsp. dried mustard
- 1/2 tsp. cayenne pepper to taste, or more
- 2 racks (4 to 5 lb.) baby back pork ribs
- 1 to 2 lemons, halved, seeded
- Hot sauce Louisiana-style, to taste

For the butter sauce:

- 8 tbsp. (1 stick) salted butter
- 1/2 cup hot sauce Louisiana-style

To serve:

- Cheese dip with Gorgonzola, recipe follows
- 4 ribs and celery, rinsed

Also you will need:

- 1 1/2 cups (preferably hickory) wood chips or chunks, soaked in water for 1 hour to cover, then drained

Directions:

1. Place the salt, lemon pepper, garlic powder, mustard, and cayenne in a small bowl and mix with your fingers, breaking up any lumps in the garlic powder or dry mustard.

2. To prepare the ribs, place a rack of ribs meat-side down on a baking sheet. Remove the thin, papery membrane from the back of the rack by inserting a slender implement, such as a butter knife or the tip of a meat thermometer under it. The best place to start is on one of the middle bones. Using a dishcloth, paper towel, or pliers to get a secure grip, peel off the membrane. Repeat with the remaining rack.

3. Sprinkle the rub over the ribs on both sides, rubbing it on the meat. On both sides, squeeze the lemon juice over the ribs, patting it with a fork. Drizzle the ribs with a tablespoon or two of hot sauce and pat them with a fork. With plastic wrap, cover the ribs and refrigerate them while making the sauces and setting up the grill.

4. To make the butter sauce, melt the butter in a saucepan over medium-high heat. Add 1/2 cup of hot sauce to the mixture and bring to a boil. Remove from the heat, then set aside the butter sauce.

5. Make the Cheese Dip with Gorgonzola, then prepare the celery. Lengthwise, cut the ribs in half, then crosswise, and cut each half into roughly 3-inch sticks. Stand the celery sticks upright in a small bowl or ramekin. To serve, refrigerate the dip and celery until ready.

6. Set up the grill for indirect grilling and preheat to medium (325 to 350°F). Place a large drip pan in the center of the grill. When ready to cook, brush, and oil the grill grate. Place the ribs, bone side down, in the center of the grate over the drip pan and away from the heat. (If your grill has limited space, stand the racks of ribs upright in a rib rack, see page...) If cooking on a charcoal grill, toss half of the wood chips on each mound of coals." The meat will have shrunk back from the ends of the bones by about 1/4 inch when the ribs are done. Brush the ribs lightly with some of the butter sauce. Rewarm if needed, two or three times after 45 minutes of cooking—a basting brush works better for this sauce than a mop. Replenish the coals as needed when using a charcoal grill. Cover the grill and cook the ribs until they are well browned, cooked through, and tender enough to pull apart with your fingers.

7. Transfer the rack of ribs to a cutting board. For a few minutes, let the ribs rest, then cut the racks into individual ribs and place them in a big bowl or arrange them on a platter. Until it is boiling, reheat the remaining butter sauce. Pour the sauce over the ribs and toss to combine. With the Gorgonzola dip and the celery, serve the ribs. Don't forget napkins.

30. Gorgonzola Dip Cheese

Ingredients:

- 3 oz. (6 tbsp.), gorgonzola cheese, rind removed, at room temperature
- 1⁄2 cup mayonnaise
- 1⁄2 cup sour cream
- 1 spoonful fresh lemon juice
- 1 large or 2 small scallions, trimmed, minced white portion, finely chopped green portions
- Coarse salt (kosher or sea) and black pepper, freshly ground

Directions:

1. In a non-reactive mixing bowl, place the cheese and mash it with a fork into a paste. Stir in the mayonnaise, sour cream, lemon juice, and white pepper. Season to taste with salt and pepper—you probably won't need much salt as the cheese is already quite salty.
2. Transfer the dip and sprinkle the chopped scallion greens on top in a nice serving bowl.

31. Julep Ribs Mint

Ingredients:

For the mint glaze:

- 3 tbsp. jelly mint
- 3 tbsp. fresh lemon juice
- 3 tbsp. salted butter
- 3 tbsp. bourbon
- 2 tbsp. sugar
- 1 tsp. liquid smoke, use only if ribs on a gas grill are cooked

For rubs and ribs:

- 2 tsp. iced tea mix, not an artificial sweetener, but made with sugar
- 2 sugar tsp.
- 2 tsp. (peppermint or spearmint) of dried mint
- 2 tsp. sweet paprika
- 2 tsp. kosher or marine coarse salt
- 1 tsp. black pepper, freshly ground
- Bourbon Mint Barbecue Sauce (recipe follows) 2 racks of baby-back pork ribs (4 to 5 lb. total)

Also, you will need:

- 1 1⁄2 cups (optional; preferably hickory) wood chips or chunks, soaked in water for 1 hour to cover, then drained

Directions:

1. To make the sauce, place the mint jelly, lemon juice, butter, bourbon, 2 tablespoons of sugar, and the liquid smoke (if used) in a small non-reactive saucepan, and stir to combine. Bring to a boil over medium heat, whisk frequently, and cook for about 5 minutes, or until the mint jelly dissolves and the glaze is syrupy. Set aside the mint glaze.

2. To make the rub, place the iced tea mix, 2 teaspoons of sugar, dried mint, paprika, salt, and pepper in a small bowl and mix with your fingers, breaking up any lumps of paprika.

3. To prepare the ribs, place a rack of ribs meat-side down on a baking sheet. Remove the thin, papery membrane from the back of the rack by inserting a slender implement, such as a butter knife or the tip of a meat thermometer under it. The best place to start is on one of the middle bones. Using a dishcloth, paper towel, or pliers to get a secure grip, peel off the membrane. Repeat with the remaining rack.

4. Sprinkle the rub over the ribs on both sides, rubbing it on the meat. While you set up the grill, cover the ribs with plastic wrap, and refrigerate them.

5. Set up the grill for indirect grilling and preheat to medium (325 to 350°F). Place a large drip pan in the center of the grill. When ready to cook, brush, and oil the grill grate. Place the ribs, bone side down, in the center of the grate over the drip pan and away from the heat. (If your grill has limited space, stand the racks of ribs upright in a rib rack, see page…) If cooking on a charcoal grill, toss half of the wood chips on each mound of coals. Cover the grill and cook the ribs for 45 minutes.

6. Cover the grill and cook the ribs for 1 hour.

7. Brush the ribs with some of the maple sauce on both sides. Re-cover the grill and continue cooking the ribs (for 15 to 30 minutes or 1 1⁄4 to 1 1⁄2) hours in total until they are well browned, cooked through, and tender enough to pull apart with your fingers. The meat will have shrunk back from the ends of the bones by about half an inch when the ribs are done. Brush the ribs with the sauce once or twice more, and if a charcoal grill is used, refill the coals as needed.

8. Transfer the ribs from the racks to a cutting board. For a few minutes, let the ribs rest, then cut the racks in half or into individual ribs. Serve with Bourbon Mint Barbecue Sauce on the side at once.

32. Bourbon Mint Barbecue Sauce

Ingredients:

- 1⁄2 cup ketchup
- 1⁄2 cup sauce with chili, see note
- 1/3 cup mint jelly
- 1⁄4 cup bourbon
- 2 tbsp. cider vinegar, or to taste
- 2 tbsp. brown sugar, or to taste
- 1 tbsp. Worcestershire sauce
- 1 tsp. smoke-based liquid
- Coarse salt (kosher or sea) and black pepper, freshly ground

Directions:

1. In a heavy non-reactive saucepan, place the ketchup, chili sauce, mint jelly, bourbon, vinegar, brown sugar, Worcestershire sauce, and liquid smoke, and stir to combine. Bring to a boil, frequently whisking, over medium heat. Reduce the heat to medium-low and let the sauce simmer gently for 8 to 10 minutes, whisking from time to time, until thick and richly flavored. Season to taste, adding a little more tartness vinegar and/or as necessary brown sugar for sweetness and salt and pepper to taste. It is possible to refrigerate the sauce, covered, for several weeks. Prior to use, let it return to room temperature.

Note: The ketchup like seasoning is the chili sauce called for here, not a tongue burner from Texas or Thailand. One brand that is good is Heinz®.

33. Memphis Slaw Mustard

Ingredients:

- 3 tbsp. Dijon mustard
- 3 tbsp. sugar
- 3 tbsp. white vinegar distilled, or to taste
- 3 tbsp. vegetable oil
- tbsp. Texas Pete® hot sauce
- Coarse salt (kosher or sea) and black pepper, freshly ground
- 1 small or 1/2 large green cabbage, cored, cut into 1-inch pieces, thinly chopped for about 4 cups
- 1 carrot, medium-size, peeled

Directions:

1. In a non-reactive mixing bowl, place the mustard and sugar and whisk to mix. Slowly whisk together the vinegar, oil, and hot sauce. Season to taste with salt and pepper—it should be highly seasoned with the dressing. Set aside the dressing.

2. In a food processor fitted with a metal chopping blade, finely chop the cabbage, running the machine in short bursts; this is a chopped, not shredded, slaw. Work in several batches so that the processor bowl does not overcrowd—overprocessing reduces the cabbage to mush. Finely grate the carrot by hand or by using the food processor's shredding disk.

3. Add the dressing to the cabbage and carrot and toss to combine. Taste for seasoning, adding salt and/or vinegar needed. Within a few hours after being made, the slaw tastes best served but can be refrigerated, covered for a day or two. Taste before serving for seasoning, add more salt and/or vinegar as needed, and toss to mix.

34. Glazed Maple-Ribs

Ingredients

For the rub and ribs:

- 2 tbsp. turbinado sugar, maple sugar, or light brown sugar
- 1 tbsp. mustard, in dry form
- 2 tsp. kosher or marine coarse salt
- 1 tsp. black pepper, freshly ground
- 1 tsp. crumbled or dried powdered sage
- 2 racks (4 to 5 lb.) baby back pork ribs

For the maple sauce:

- 1 cup real syrup with maple
- Ketchup with 3 tbsp.
- 2 tbsp. sauce from Worcestershire
- 1 tbsp. Mustard Dijon
- 1 tbsp. vinegar with cider
- 1 tbsp. horseradish prepared
- 1⁄2 cup sugar from maple or turbinado sugar

Also, you will need:

- 11⁄2 cups wood chips or chunks, soaked in water for 1 hour to cover, then drained

Directions:

1. To make the rub, place the maple sugar, dry mustard, salt, pepper, and sage in a small bowl, and sage and mix with your fingers, breaking up any lumps in the dry mustard or maple sugar.

2. To prepare the ribs, place a rack of ribs meat-side down on a baking sheet. Remove the thin, papery membrane from the back of the rack by inserting a slender implement, such as a butter knife or the tip of a meat thermometer under it. The best place to start is on one of the middle bones. Using a dishcloth, paper towel, or pliers to get a secure grip, peel off the membrane. Repeat with the remaining rack.

3. Sprinkle the rub over the ribs on both sides, rubbing it on the meat. Cover and refrigerate the ribs with plastic wrap while you make the glaze and set up the grill.

4. To make the sauce, place the maple syrup, ketchup, Worcestershire sauce, Dijon mustard, vinegar, and horseradish in a heavy non-reactive saucepan. Bring to a boil, whisking to combine, over high heat. Reduce the heat to medium and let the glaze simmer 3 to 5 minutes, whisking as needed, until thick and syrupy. Set aside the sauce.

5. Set up the grill for indirect grilling and preheat to medium (325 to 350°F). Place a large drip pan in the center of the grill. When ready to cook, brush, and oil the grill grate. Place the ribs, bone side down, in the center of the grate over the drip pan and away from the heat. (If your grill has limited space, stand the racks of ribs upright in a rib rack, see page…) If cooking on a charcoal grill, toss half of the wood chips on each mound of coals. Cover the grill and cook the ribs for 45 minutes.

6. Brush the ribs with some of the maple sauce on both sides. Re-cover the grill and continue cooking the ribs (for 30 to 45 minutes or 1 1/4 to 1 1/2) hours in total until they are well browned, cooked through, and tender enough to pull apart with your fingers. The meat will have shrunk back from the ends of the bones by about 1/4 inch when the ribs are done. Brush the ribs with the sauce once or twice more and replenish the coals as needed when using a charcoal grill.

7. Brush the ribs once again with maple sauce on both sides just before serving and sprinkle both sides with the maple sugar. Move the ribs directly over the fire and grill 1 to 3 minutes per side, or until the sauce is browned and caramelized.

8. Transfer the ribs to a large platter or cutting board. For a few minutes, let the ribs rest, then cut the racks in half or into individual ribs. With any remaining maple glaze on the side, serve at once.

35. Rendezvous Ribs Ribsus

Ingredients:

- 1/3 cup sweet paprika
- 2 spoonfuls chili powder
- 1 tbsp. powdered garlic
- 1 tbsp. dried oregano, preferably Greek
- 1 tbsp. kosher or marine coarse salt
- 2 tsp. coarsely ground black pepper
- 2 spoonfuls mustard seeds
- 1 tsp. seed celery
- 1 cup white vinegar, distilled
- 2 racks (4 to 5 lb.) baby back pork ribs
- Memphis Mustard Slaw for serving (recipe follows)

Directions:

1. Place the paprika, chili powder, garlic powder, oregano, salt, pepper, mustard seeds, and the celery seeds in a small bowl and mix them with your fingers, breaking up any lumps. Set aside the seasoning mixture.
2. Add 2 tablespoons of the seasoning mixture and 1 cup of water, place the vinegar in a non-reactive bowl and whisk until the ingredients dissolve. Set the mop sauce aside.
3. To prepare the ribs, place a rack of ribs meat-side down on a baking sheet. Remove the thin, papery membrane from the back of the rack by inserting a slender implement, such as a butter knife or the tip of a meat thermometer under it. The best place to start is on one of the middle bones. Using a dishcloth, paper towel, or pliers to get a secure grip, peel off the membrane. Repeat with the remaining rack.

4. Set up the grill for indirect grilling and preheat to medium (325 to 350°F). Place a large drip pan in the center of the grill. When ready to cook, brush, and oil the grill grate. Place the ribs, bone side down, in the center of the grate over the drip pan and away from the heat. (If your grill has limited space, stand the racks of ribs upright in a rib rack, see page...) If cooking on a charcoal grill, toss half of the wood chips on each mound of coals. Cover the grill and cook the ribs for 30 minutes.

5. Brush the ribs with some of the maple sauce on both sides. Re-cover the grill and continue cooking the ribs for 45 minutes to 1 hour (or 1 1/4 to 1 1/2 hours in total), or until they are well browned, cooked through, and tender enough to pull apart with your fingers. The meat would have shrunk back from the ends of the bones by around 1/4 inch when the ribs are finished. Mop them again after the ribs have cooked for an hour and if you use a charcoal grill, replenish the coals as needed.

6. Move the ribs straight over the heat just before serving and grill them until brown and sizzling, 1 to 3 minutes on each side.

7. Transfer the ribs to a large platter or cutting board. Let the ribs rest for a few minutes, then use the remaining mop sauce to generously mop each rack of ribs. Cut the racks into individual ribs or in half. Sprinkle some of the residual seasoning mixtures thickly on top. Serve with the mustard slaw at once.

36. Chinatown Ribs

Ingredients:

- 1 cup Hoisin Sauce®
- 1⁄2 cup sugar
- 1⁄2 a tsp. five-spice Chinese powder

For the sauce:

- 1/3 cup dry sherry or Chinese rice wine
- 3 tbsp. sesame oil from Asia, dark
- 5 garlic cloves, peeled, gently crushed with a cleaver
- 5 (1⁄4-inch thick) fresh ginger slices peeled and gently crushed with a cleaver
- 3 scallions, trimmed, white parts gently crushed with cleaver side, green parts gently crushed with a cleaver
- 2 (4 to 5 lb.) racks baby back pork ribs

Also you will need:

- 1 1⁄2 cups (preferably cherry) wood chips or chunks, immersed in water for 1 hour to cover, then drained

Directions:

1. In a non-reactive blending cup, put the hoisin sauce, sugar, and five-spice powder and whisk to combine. Add the soy sauce, sesame oil, and rice wine, and whisk until the sugar is dissolved. Stir in the garlic, white ginger, and white scallions. To make a sauce, set 1/3 of the marinade aside.

2. To prepare the ribs, place a rack of ribs meat-side down on a baking sheet. Remove the thin, papery membrane from the back of the rack by inserting a slender implement, such as a butter knife or the tip of a meat thermometer under it. The best place to start is on one of the middle bones. Using a dishcloth, paper towel, or pliers to get a secure grip, peel off the membrane. Repeat with the remaining rack.

3. Place the ribs just large enough to hold them in a non-reactive roasting pan or baking dish. Pour the remaining marinade over the ribs and spread it with a rubber spatula all over the shelves, turning both sides to cover. Let the ribs marinate, covered, for at least 4 hours in the refrigerator or until overnight, turning 3 or 4 times. The longer the ribs marinate, the richer the taste will be— the ribs can also be marinated in large, heavy, re-sealable plastic bags.

4. Set up the grill for indirect grilling and preheat to medium (325 to 350°F). Place a large drip pan in the center of the grill. When ready to cook, brush, and oil the grill grate. Place the ribs, bone side down, in the center of the grate over the drip pan and away from the heat. (If your grill has limited space, stand the racks of ribs upright in a rib rack, see page...) If cooking on a charcoal grill, toss half of the wood chips on each mound of coals. Cover the grill and cook the ribs for 1 ¼ to 1 1/2, or until dark brown and very crisp on the outside and tender enough for your fingers to pull them apart. The meat will have shrunk back from the ends of the bones by about 1⁄4 inch when the ribs are done. Replenish the coals as needed when using a charcoal grill.

5. Meanwhile, in a non-reactive saucepan, transfer the reserved marinade, let it simmer over medium heat, and cook until thick and flavorful, about 3 minutes. Let cool the resulting sauce to room temperature, then strain it into a nice bowl for serving.

6. Transfer the ribs to a large platter or cutting board. For a few minutes, let the ribs rest, then cut the racks in half or into individual ribs. Brush or drizzle some of the sauce over the ribs and sprinkle on top with the scallion greens. With the remaining sauce on the side, serve at once.

37. Baby Backs Buccaneer

Ingredients:

- 1 large orange
- 1 small, coarsely chopped onion
- 2 garlic cloves, coarsely chopped
- 1⁄2 bunch chives, or 2 scallions, cut and coarsely chopped, both white and green (3 to 4 tbsp.)
- 1⁄2 to 1 chili Scotch bonnet, seeded and minced
- 2 tbsp. fresh flat-leaf parsley coarsely chopped
- 3 tsp. vinegar, for red wine
- 3 spoonfuls soy sauce
- 3 tbsp. vegetable oil
- 1⁄2 tsp. black pepper, freshly ground
- 4 allspice berries, or 1⁄4 tsp. allspice ground
- 1⁄4 tsp. whole or ground cloves
- Rumbullion Barbecue Sauce
- 2 (4 to 5 lb. total) racks baby back pork ribs

Also you will need:

1. 1 1⁄2 cups (preferably apple or cherry) wood chips or chunks, immersed in water for 1 hour to cover, then drained
2. Remove 2 strips of orange zest (the oil-rich outer rind) using a vegetable peeler. Place them in a food processor or blender's bowl. Halve the orange and squeeze the juice out, discarding any seeds. For the Rumbullion Barbecue Sauce, set 2 tablespoons of orange juice aside and apply the remaining orange juice to the marinade food processor.

3. In the food processor and puree, add the onion, garlic, chives, Scotch bonnet, parsley, vinegar, soy sauce, oil, pepper, allspice, and cloves until smooth.

Directions:

1. To prepare the ribs, place a rack of ribs meat-side down on a baking sheet. Remove the thin, papery membrane from the back of the rack by inserting a slender implement, such as a butter knife or the tip of a meat thermometer under it. The best place to start is on one of the middle bones. Using a dishcloth, paper towel, or pliers to get a secure grip, peel off the membrane. Repeat with the remaining rack.

2. Place the ribs and pour the marinade over them in a large non-reactive roasting pan or baking dish, turning the racks to cover both sides. Let the ribs marinate in the refrigerator, covered, for at least 6 hours or as long as 24 hours, turning 3 or 4 times. The longer the ribs marinate, the richer the taste would be—the ribs can also be marinated in a large, heavy, re-sealable plastic bags.

3. Set up the grill for indirect grilling and preheat to medium (325° to 350°F). Place a large drip pan in the center of the grill. When ready to cook, brush, and oil the grill grate. Place the ribs, bone side down, in the center of the grate over the drip pan and away from the heat. (If your grill has limited space, stand the racks of ribs upright in a rib rack, see page...) If cooking on a charcoal grill, toss half of the wood chips on each mound of coals. Cover the grill and cook the ribs for 1 ¼ to 1 ½ or until tender. They will be handsomely browned when the ribs are cooked, and the meat will have shrunk back by around 1/4 inch from the ends of the bones. Replenish the coals as needed when using a charcoal grill.

4. Brush the ribs on both sides lightly with a little of the Rumbullion Barbecue Sauce just before serving. Move the ribs directly over the fire and grill for 1 to 3 minutes per side, or until the sauce is sizzling and browned.

5. Transfer the ribs to a large platter or cutting board. For a few minutes, let the ribs rest, then split the racks in half or into individual ribs. On the side, serve the remaining barbecue sauce.

38. Rumbullion Barbecue Sauce

Ingredients:

- 1/4 cup dark rum, or taste
- 1/4 cup honey
- 1/4 cup dark brown sugar tightly packed, or to taste
- 1/4 cup fresh, or more to taste, lime juice
- 3 tbsp. soy sauce, or to taste
- 2 tbsp. fresh orange juice
- Buccaneer Baby Backs, reserved
- 1/2 tsp. cinnamon ground
- 1/2 tsp. ground nutmeg
- 1 cup ketchup

Directions:

1. In a large non-reactive saucepan, put the rum, honey, brown sugar, lime juice, soy sauce, orange juice, cinnamon, and nutmeg and bring it to a boil over high heat. Reduce the heat to medium and allow the mixture to simmer, 3 to 5 minutes, or until syrupy.

2. Stir in 2 to 3 tablespoons of water and the ketchup and let the sauce simmer gently for 6 to 10 minutes until thick and aromatic. "Taste for seasoning, if a saltier flavor is desired, adding more soy sauce, more brown sugar; if sweetness is desired, more lime juice; if tartness is desired, and more rum if you agree with the claim of Mark Twain that too much liquor is nearly enough.

3. Prior to serving, let the sauce cool to room temperature. It can be refrigerated for several weeks, sealed. Before serving, let it return to room temperature.

CHAPTER 3: BEEF RECIPES

39. Flank Steak Barbecued

Ingredients:

- Olive oil for 1/2 cup

- 1 onion, medium-sized, thinly sliced

- 3 garlic cloves, finely chopped

- 3 serrano chilies, seeded and finely chopped

- 2 tsp. fresh cilantro, chopped

- 1/2 cup fresh lime juice with 1 tbsp. salt

- 1 (1 1/4 lb. or so) flank steak

- 1 1/2 cups barbecue sauce

- bacon fat (recipe follows)

- Warm tortillas

Directions:

1. In a big, shallow dish, combine the olive oil, onion, garlic, chili, cilantro, lime juice, and salt. Add the flank steak and marinate for 8 hours or overnight in the refrigerator, turning from time to time.

2. Heat a grill, and if needed, add wood chips. Coat the flank steak with the marinade and place on the hot grill. Cook for 3 minutes. Turn it around and cook for three minutes. Use a brush to coat a flank with some of the barbecue sauce. Switch to the other side and powder it. Continue to cook, brush with the sauce, and turn every 3 minutes until the meat is medium-rare, approximately 18 minutes in total.

3. Slice the meat into thin strips over the grain. Serve with hot tortillas, Grilled- Guacamole Onion, and watermelon pico de gallo.

40. Barbecue Bacon Fat Sauce

Ingredients:

- 1 tbsp. fat or vegetable oil, for bacon
- 1 big yellow onion, sliced into 1⁄4-inch cubes
- 1 cup ketchup for
- 1⁄4 cup Worcestershire sauce
- 1 tbsp. vinegar, for malt
- 2 tbsp. molasses
- 2 tsp. creole mustard
- 1 tsp. red pepper hot sauce
- 1⁄2 tsp. salt, or to taste
- 1 tsp. fresh lemon juice, or to taste

Directions:

1. Place the fat or oil in a medium saucepan over medium heat.
2. Add the onion and cook for about 5 minutes, until tender.
3. Add the remaining ingredients and stir. Boil for 15 minutes. Keep warm till you are ready to serve.

41. Bulgogi (Barbecued Beef from Korea)

Ingredients:

- 1 1/2 lb. tenderloin or flank steak of beef
- 3 1/2 spoonfuls soy sauce
- 1 1/2 tbsp. sugar
- 5 tbsp. scallions, diagonally chopped
- 1 tsp. garlic minced
- 11/2 tbsp. crushed sesame seeds toasted
- 1 large onion, sliced thinly
- 2 tbsp. sesame oil
- 2 spoonfuls rice wine
- 1/4 tsp. black pepper
- 2 spoonfuls sherry

Directions:

1. Cut beef into bits that are 1 1/2 inches square and 1/8 inch thick. When partially frozen, it is best to slice the meat thinly.
2. Combine the beef with other ingredients.
3. Grill all the slices of meat and onion over a charcoal fire until the outside is just brown and the inside is pink. It's going to take 2 to 4 minutes.

42. Tacos Grilled Carne Asada

Ingredients:

- 1 garlic clove, peeled
- 2 kilos skirt steak
- 2 tsp. cumin field
- 1 tsp. oregano ground
- 1/2 tsp. cayenne pepper
- Salt and black pepper freshly ground

Directions:

1. Startup a grill with charcoal or gas. Crush the garlic and rub the steak with it. Mix the remaining ingredients and add them to the steak. Let the steak sit till you're ready for grilling.

2. For medium-rare, grill the steak 3 to 4 minutes on each side—hot is best but mild or room temperature is fine. Cut into slices and use as soon as possible.

43. Sandwich with Baltimore Pit Beef

Ingredients:

For the rub:

- 2 tsp. salt seasoned
- 1 tbsp. sweet paprika
- 1 tsp. powdered garlic
- 1 tsp. dried oregano
- 1/2 tsp. black pepper

For the sandwich:

- 1 (3-lb.) top-round bit
- 8 kaiser rolls or 16 Horseradish sauce rye bread slices (recipe follows)
- 1 sweet white onion, thinly sliced
- 2 ripe tomatoes, sliced thinly, optional
- Lettuce from Ice burg, optional

Directions:

1. In a bowl, combine the rub ingredients and blend. Sprinkle 3 to 4 tbsp. of beef all over and pat it in. Place and cover with plastic wrap in a baking dish. You can cover the beef with the rub for a few hours, but leave it in the refrigerator for 3 days for full flavor, turning once a day.
2. Get the hot grill packed. Grill the beef for 30 to 40 minutes or until it is crusty and dark brown outside and the temperature inside is around 120°F for rare. Switch the beef around sometimes. Transfer to a cutting board and leave for 5 minutes to rest.

3. Thinly, slice the beef through the grain, high on a roll or bread pile of beef slathered with horseradish sauce. Attach the onion, tomatoes, and sliced lettuce to garnish. Just serve.

44. Smoky Brisket

Ingredients:

- 1 (4 lb.) brisket bit

For the dry mop:

- 1⁄2 cup sweet paprika
- 3 tbsp. salt
- 2 spoonful pepper, freshly ground

For the wet mop:

- 2⁄3 a cup water
- 1 1⁄2 tbsp. instant espresso crystals
- 2 cups ketchup
- 3⁄4 cup Worcestershire sauce
- 1⁄4 lb. (1 stick) butter

For the barbecue sauce:

- 1 pureéd, medium-size onion
- 1⁄4 cup olive oil
- 4 1⁄3 cups tomato purée with 2 cups water
- 2 bay leaves
- 3⁄4 cup dark brown sugar
- 2 cubes bouillon Beef
- 3 tsp. hot pepper sauce, including Tabasco® sauce
- 2 spoonfuls chili powder

- 1 tbsp. cayenne pepper
- 1 spoonful pure lemon juice
- 3/4 tsp. freshly ground pepper
- 1/4 tsp. salt
- 1/3 cup vinegar, for cider

Directions:

1. To make a dry mop, combine the ingredients for the dry mop. Rub the brisket all over. Set aside.

2. To prepare a wet mop, mix the wet mop ingredients in a small saucepan, except for the butter. Just bring it to a boil. Reduce the heat and simmer for 20 minutes. Remove from heat and add butter and whisk and set aside.

3. Slowly grill the brisket for 2 hours, basting with a wet mop every 30 minutes.

4. In the meantime, make a barbecue sauce. In a saucepan, combine the onion purée and the olive oil. Sauté for about 5 minutes until translucent. Add the remaining ingredients, with the exception of the vinegar, bring to a simmer over low heat and simmer for 20 minutes. Remove from the oven, add the vinegar, and stir.

5. Cut the brisket into thin slices and serve with barbecue sauce.

45. Steak Au Poivre Barbecued

Ingredients:

- 3 (1 1/2-pound) boneless shell steaks, trimmed with excess fat and gently pounded, about 3 inches thick
- 1 tbsp. coarse salt
- 1/4 cup crushed or half black, half white, if desired, black peppercorns
- 1/4 cup shallots finely chopped
- 1/2 cup dry red wine
- 1/2 cup beef stock, homemade or frozen
- 4 tbsp. (1/2 stick), unsalted butter, at room temperature

Directions:

1. Steaks with dust and coarse salt. On a flat surface, laid crushed peppercorns and pressed steaks over them to coat on all sides.
2. Grill the steaks for around 20 minutes. The easiest way to cook is to sear for about 4 minutes on one side, then flip and sear for 4 minutes on the other side. The flat rim must also be seared for several minutes by standing steaks on their sides. Continue to rotate until the steaks hit the necessary density.
3. When barbecuing steaks, mix shallots, red wine, and beef stock in a saucepan. Reducing to 1/3 of the volume over medium-high heat. On a warm, serving platter, remove the cooked steaks. Apply some butter to the sauce and pour over the steaks. Slice the biased steaks into a bowl, allowing the juices to mix with the sauce.

Note: Use a heavy, flat-bottomed skillet to crush peppercorns by putting them on the flat, hard surface and gently cracking them.

46. Grilled Flank Steak

Ingredients:

- 1⁄2 cup whiskey
- 1⁄2 cup sauce, for soy
- 1 1⁄2 lb. steak flank

Directions:

1. Whisk together the bourbon, soy sauce, and 1⁄2 cup of water in a small bowl to make a marinade. Pour the marinade into a 1-gallon, self-sealing food storage bag. Put the steak in the bag and turn it over several times to cover the whole cut. Marinate for 2 hours in the refrigerator, turning the steak once every hour. Pour the marinade off and dry the steak with paper towels.

2. Prepare the grill for a fire. Grill the steak for 4 minutes on one side for rare, 5 minutes for medium-rare, until flames have subsided and coals are burning away. Switch on the steak and grill for another 3 to 4 minutes to taste.

3. Move the steak to a cutting board, cover it lightly with foil and let it rest for 5 minutes. Cross-slice the steak into 1⁄8-inch-thick slices.

47. Beef Ribs on Salt and Pepper

Ingredients:

- 2 (5 to 6 lb.) racks long beef ribs
- Coarse (kosher or sea) salt
- (not finely ground) Crushed black peppercorns
- (optional; for spicier ribs) Spicy red pepper flakes
- Bunker Blaster Sauce for Barbecue

Also, you will need:

- 1 1/2 cups (preferably oak) wood chips or chunks, immersed in water for 1 hour to cover, then drained

Directions:

1. To prepare the ribs, place a rack of ribs meat-side down on a baking sheet. Remove the thin, papery membrane from the back of the rack by inserting a slender implement, such as a butter knife or the tip of a meat thermometer under it. The best place to start is on one of the middle bones. Using a dishcloth, paper towel, or pliers to get a secure grip, peel off the membrane. Repeat with the remaining rack.

2. Season the ribs generously with salt, cracked black pepper, and hot pepper flakes, if used on both sides. While you set up the grill, cover the ribs with plastic wrap, and refrigerate them.

3. Set up the grill for indirect grilling and preheat to medium (325° to 350°F). Place a large drip pan in the center of the grill. When ready to cook, brush, and oil the grill grate. Place the ribs, bone-side down, in the center of the grate over the drip pan and away from the heat. Cover the grill and cook the ribs until they are well browned, cooked through, and soft enough for tour fingers to pull them apart—1 1/2 to 2 hours in total. The meat would have shrunk back

from the ends of the bones by around 1/4 inch when the ribs are finished. Replenish the coals as needed when using a charcoal grill.

4. Move the ribs to a wide platter or cutting board, and let them rest for a few minutes. If you serve 4, break the racks in half or into 1 or 2-rib sections. Serve with the Bunker Blaster Barbecue Sauce all at once.

48. Bunker Blaster Sauce of Barbecue

Ingredients:

- 2 1/4 cups ketchup
- 1/2 cup molasses
- 1/4 cup vinegar with white wine
- 1 1/2 tsp. smoking oil
- 2 tsp. fresh onion minced
- 2 tbsp. brown sugar
- 1/4 tsp. coarse kosher or sea salt
- ½ tsp. chili powder
- 1/4 tsp. powder onion
- 1/4 tsp. powdered garlic
- 1/8 tsp. cayenne pepper

Directions:

1. In a strong non-reactive saucepan, put the ketchup, molasses, vinegar, liquid smoke, onion, brown sugar, salt, chili powder, onion and garlic powder, and cayenne, and whisk to combine.
2. Gradually, bring the sauce to a boil over medium heat, whisking as needed.
3. Reduce the heat slightly and let the sauce simmer for about 10 minutes, until it is thick and richly flavored—the sauce can be refrigerated in a clean jar for several months prior to use. Let it return to room temperature.

49. Lone Star Beef Ribs

Ingredients:

For the rib rub and for the Lone Star:

- 3 tbsp. kosher or marine coarse salt
- 3 tbsp. pure powdered chili
- 1 tbsp. black cracked pepper
- 2 tsp. powdered garlic
- 2 dried oregano tsp.
- 1 cayenne pepper tsp.
- 1 tsp. cumin field

For the mop sauce:

- 1 Lone Star beer bottle or other lager-style beer
- 1⁄2 cup white vinegar, distillated
- 1⁄2 cup coffee brewed
- 2 (5 to 6 lb. total) racks of long beef ribs, beef back ribs
- Bare-bones, for barbecue sauce (page...)

Also, you will need:

- 1 1⁄2 cups (preferably oak) wood chips or chunks, immersed in water for 1 hour to cover, then drained the barbecue mop

Directions:

4. Place the salt, chili powder, cracked pepper, garlic powder, oregano, cayenne, and cumin in a small bowl and blend with your fingers. Make the Lone Star rib rub: For the Bare-Bones Barbecue Sauce, set aside 1 tablespoon of the rub.

5. Make the mop sauce: Place in a non-reactive bowl the beer, vinegar, coffee, and 1½ tablespoons of the Lone Star rib rub and whisk to mix. Set the mop sauce separately and the remaining rub aside.

6. To prepare the ribs, place a rack of ribs meat-side down on a baking sheet. Remove the thin, papery membrane from the back of the rack by inserting a slender implement, such as a butter knife or the tip of a meat thermometer under it. The best place to start is on one of the middle bones. Using a dishcloth, paper towel, or pliers to get a secure grip, peel off the membrane. Repeat with the remaining rack.

7. Sprinkle the ribs generously with the remaining rub on both sides, using around 1 tablespoon per side and rubbing it on the meat. (Any leftover rub will be kept away from heat and light in a sealed jar for several weeks.) Cover the ribs with plastic wrap and refrigerate them under the grill while you set up the grill.

8. Set up the grill for indirect grilling and preheat to medium (325° to 350°F). Place a large drip pan in the center of the grill. When ready to cook, brush, and oil the grill grate. Place the ribs, bone-side down, in the center of the grate over the drip pan and away from the heat. (If your grill has limited space, stand the racks of ribs upright in a rib rack, see page...) If cooking on a charcoal grill, toss half of the wood chips on each mound of coals. Cover the grill and cook the ribs for 45 minutes.

9. Brush the ribs with some of the mop sauce on both sides. Re-cover the grill and continue cooking the ribs (for 30 to 45 minutes or 1 1/4 to 1 1/2) hours in total until they are well browned, cooked through, and tender enough to pull them apart with your fingers. The meat would have shrunk back from the ends of the bones by around 1/4 inch when the ribs are finished. Once or twice more, mop the ribs and refill the coals as required.

10. Transfer the ribs to a large cutting board or platter and leave for a few minutes to rest. Save the drippings for the Bare-Bones Barbecue Sauce from the ribs where appropriate (see Note). If you need 4 servings, split the racks in half or into 1 or 2 rib sections. Serve with the barbecue sauce at once.

50. Sake-Short Grilled Ribs

Ingredients:

- 1 bunch white and green scallions, trimmed, coarsely chopped
- 3 tbsp. scallion greens
- 6 garlic cloves, coarsely chopped
- 3 to 6 (1⁄2 cup) shallots, coarsely chopped
- 1 slice (2 inches), fresh ginger, peeled, coarsely chopped
- 1⁄2 cup sake, or as required
- 12 (about 4 lb. total) bone-in individual beef short ribs
- Pac-Rim Barbecue Sauce, recipe follows
- kosher or coarse sea salt and freshly ground black pepper

Also you will need:

- 9 x11-inch aluminum foil pan
- 12 (12-inch) bamboo skewers

Directions:

1. In a food processor, put the scallions, garlic, shallots, and ginger and chop them finely. Add 1⁄2 cup of sake with the motor working, or enough to get a thick paste. With salt and pepper to taste, season this wet rub.

2. Season the ribs generously with salt and pepper on both sides.

3. Sprinkle the bottom of the aluminum foil pan with a third of the wet rub. Using a spatula, place 6 ribs on top and spread half of the remaining wet rub over them. On top, arrange the remaining ribs

and distribute the rest of the wet rub over them. Cover the pan with aluminum foil, creating a strong seal by crimping the sides.

4. Make the Barbecue Sauce Pac-Rim.

5. For indirect grilling, set up the grill (see page…) and preheat it to medium-low (300°F).

6. Place the pan away from the heat with the ribs in the center of the grill and cover the grill. For 2 hours, cook the ribs. Then remove the aluminum foil, cover the grill again and cook the ribs until very tender and deep golden brown for 1 to 2 hours or 3 to 4 hours in total. You should be able to pick the meat off the rib bones with a fork when finished—replenish the coals as needed if using a charcoal grill.

7. Brush the ribs all over with Pac-Rim Barbecue Sauce just before serving and move them directly across the pit. Grill on all sides until sizzling and browned, or 1 to 2 minutes per side, 4 to 8 minutes in total.

8. Move the ribs to a platter or plates and sprinkle over them with the reserved scallion greens. With the remaining Pac-Rim Barbecue Sauce on the side, serve at once.

51. Koreatown Short Beef Ribs (The KALBI KUI)

Ingredients:

For the ribs and marinade:

- 3 lb. bone-in short beef ribs, preferably in strips
- 4 garlic cloves, minced
- 1⁄4 cup sugar
- 1⁄2 cup sauce for soy
- 1⁄4 cup Asian dark sesame
- 1 tsp. black pepper, freshly ground

For the "Yang-Nyum Jang" dipping sauce:

- 1 garlic clove, minced
- 2 tsp. sugar
- 1⁄4 cup soy sauce
- 1⁄2 tsp. black pepper, freshly ground

To serve:

- 6 garlic cloves, thinly sliced
- 2 jalapeño peppers, thinly crosswise sliced
- 2 medium-sized heads Roman lettuce, split into whole leaves, rinsed and spun dry
- 1⁄2 cup Korean hot bean paste
- Korean Salad with Cucumber
- Rice Sticky

Also you will need:

- A vegetable grating (sometimes referred to as a grilling grid)

Directions:

1. To prepare the short ribs, place a short-short rib on the side of the meat on the work surface. By running a sharp knife between the top of the bone and the fleshy part of the beef, trim the meat off the rib. You'll end up with a piece of beef. Thinly slice the meat sharply on the diagonal with the grain, beginning with the long end. The definition is to cut meat slices that are 1 1/2 to 2 inches wide, 2 to 3 inches long, and around 1/8 inch thick. Put aside the bone that will be added to either side with a little meat. Repeat with the short ribs that remain.

2. To make the marinade, put the four minced garlic cloves and 1/4 cup of sugar in a mixing bowl, and mash them with the back of a wooden. Add 1/2 cup of the sesame oil and soy sauce and 1 teaspoon of the black pepper; stir to blend. Stir in the short, sliced rib meat and the bones. Let the short ribs marinate, wrapped, for 2 to 4 hours in the refrigerator.

3. To make the dipping sauce, put the remaining minced garlic clove and 2 tablespoons of sugar in a mixing bowl and mash with the back of a wooden spoon. Add 1/4 of a cup of soy sauce, 1/2 of a teaspoon of black pepper, and 1/4 of a bottle of water. For serving, divide the dipping sauce into 4 small bowls.

4. Place the sliced garlic and jalapeños in small bowls shortly before you're ready to begin grilling. On a tray, arrange the lettuce leaves. If used, put the hot bean paste and the cucumber and rice lettuce in separate bowls, each with a serving spoon. To keep it soft, cover the rice.

5. Set up the grill for direct grilling (see page ... you'll be using a charcoal-burning hibachi in the best of both worlds). Preheat the grill to high; to verify the heat, use the Mississippi test (see page...). On the rack grill, put the vegetable gratin and preheat it as well.

6. Lightly oil the vegetable griddle when ready to cook, using a folded paper towel dipped in vegetable oil and gripping it with tongs.

7. In the vegetable griddle, arrange the beef bones and some of the beef slices. Grill until cooked to taste, 2 to 4 minutes for medium-well on each side (Koreans like their beef ribs pretty well done), or turn with tongs or chopsticks to taste. It's going to take a little longer for the bones; they should be perfectly browned, with sizzling meat on the sides. Arrange some of the garlic and jalapeño slices on the vegetable griddle after turning the beef and cook until lightly browned, 1 minute on each side. Serve the beef, garlic, and jalapeños on the grill, and then proceed to cook more meat, garlic, and jalapeños.

8. Spread a lettuce leaf with a little of the hot bean paste to each kalbi kui (if used) and top it with rice. On the rice, put a few slices of grilled meat and top it with some cucumber salad and slices of grilled garlic and jalapeño. Roll up the lettuce leaf like a taco and dip it in the dipping sauce cup. To gnaw on, eat the grilled bones separately.

52. Grandpa's Barbecued Short Ribs Pastrami

Ingredients:

For the ribs and the rub:

- 3 to 4 lb. short ribs, bone-in beef
- 3 tbsp. cilantro seeds
- 2 1/2 tsp. peppercorns black
- 2 whole star anise, torn to bits, or 1 tsp. ground anise
- 2 spoonfuls mustard seeds
- 3 tbsp. dark brown sugar
- 1 broad head of garlic (8 to 10 cloves), broken, peeled, and coarsely chopped into individual cloves
- 2 tbsp. kosher or marine coarse salt
- 1 to 2 tbsp. canola or other vegetable oil

For the mop sauce:

- 1 cup ale of ginger
- 1/2 cup vinegar with cider
- 1 tsp. coarse (kosher or sea) salt
- Your favorite barbecue sauce for serving

Also, you will need:

- 1 1/2 cups wood chips or chunks, immersed in water for 1 hour to cover them, then drained

Directions:

1. To prepare the ribs, deeply score the meaty top part of each rib in a crosshatch pattern using a sharp knife. The cuts should be roughly 1⁄2 inch deep and 1⁄2 inch apart. Place the ribs in a non-reactive roasting pan. Place the coriander seeds, peppercorns, anise, mustard seeds, and brown sugar in a mortar and, using a pestle, pound them until they are crushed coarsely.

2. Or in a food processor equipped with a metal blade, you can smash them, working the system in short bursts. Pound the garlic and the 2 tablespoons of salt in or purée it. To obtain a thick paste, add ample oil.

3. Spread the wet rub over the ribs on all sides using a spatula. Tightly cover the ribs with plastic wrap and let them marinate for at least 12 hours or overnight in the refrigerator. Make the mop sauce right before you intend to grill.

4. In a small non-reactive cup, place the ginger ale, vinegar, and 1 teaspoon salt and whisk until the salt dissolves. Place the mop sauce aside. For indirect grilling, set up a charcoal grill and preheat it to medium (325 to 350°F).

5. Place a large drip pan under the grid in the middle of the grill. Brush and oil the grill grate when ready to cook. In the center of the grater, put the ribs bone side down over the drip pan and away from the sun.

6. Toss the coals with wood chips. Cover the grill and cook for 45 minutes with the ribs. With the mop sauce, baste the ribs on both sides. Re-cover the grill and continue to cook the ribs for 45 minutes to 1 1⁄4 hours (1 1⁄2 to 2 hours in total), or until cooked through and very tender. Mop the ribs once or twice more and wrap them with aluminum foil if they tend to brown too much after 1 1⁄2 hours. As required, replenish the coals. Move the ribs to a dish or plate and leave for a few minutes to rest. With the barbecue sauce of your choice, serve the ribs.

53. Short Ribs Argentinean

Ingredients:

- 1 tbsp. kosher or marine coarse salt
- 1 tbsp. oregano, dried
- 1 tsp. black pepper, freshly ground
- 1 tsp. red pepper spicy flakes
- 2 garlic cloves s, minced
- Short ribs of around 3 lb. bone-in beef, cut crosswise into long, 1⁄2-inch-wide strips
- 1 to 2 tsp. olive oil
- Chimichurri Sauce

Directions:

1. Make a rub with chimichurri.
2. In a small bowl, put the salt, oregano, black pepper, hot pepper flakes, and garlic and mix them. In a baking dish, put the short ribs. Sprinkle both sides of the ribs with the chimichurri rub, rubbing it on the beef. Lightly drizzle olive oil on both sides over the ribs, rubbing it on the meat. Cover and refrigerate the ribs with plastic wrap as you make the sauce and set up the grill. Create and set aside the Chimichurri Sauce.
3. Set up the grill for direct grilling and preheat it to high—check the heat using the Mississippi test. Brush and oil the grill grate when ready to cook. Place the short ribs on the grill and cook until the outside is sizzling and darkly browned and cooked to taste, about 3 to 5 minutes on each side for medium.
4. Move the ribs to a bowl or dish and leave for a few minutes to rest. Serve the ribs with the Chimichurri sauce spooned over them.

CHAPTER 4: SEAFOOD RECIPES

54. Charcoal-Grilled Bass Striped

Ingredients:

- 1 striped (3- to 4 lb.) bass, gutted
- Salt and black pepper freshly ground
- 1 garlic clove, peeled
- 1 fresh rosemary sprig, large
- 1 bay leaf
- Oil
- 1/4 lb. (1 stick) butter, melted and held hot
- 1/4 cup fresh chopped parsley lemon wedges

Directions:

1. Have a charcoal fire ready—they are ready when white ash forms on top of the coals.
2. Meanwhile, get the fish packed. With salt and pepper, rub it inside and out. Break a clove of garlic into slivers. Make a few small incisions along the backbone of the fish using a sharp paring knife. Insert garlic slivers.
3. Set the rosemary sprig and the bay leaf in the fish cavity. Tie the fish with strings in two or three positions to protect the cavity. Rub the fish generously with oil all over. Place the fish on the hot grill and cook on one side for 10 to 15 minutes, rubbing occasionally with butter. Loosen the fish from the grill using a pancake turner or spatula, or both, and turn it to the other side. On that side, cook for 10 to 15 minutes or until the fish is finished and the meat

flakes easily when checked with a fork. Cooking time will depend on the size of the fish, heat strength, and how close the coals are to the fish.

4. Move the fish to a hot dish and pour in the remaining butter. Garnish with lemon wedges and sprinkle with parsley.

55. Fish with marinated tomatoes in Greek-Style

Ingredients:

- 2 cups cherry tomatoes, Sun Gold preferably, halved
- 4 tbsp. olive oil, or as needed
- 2 tbsp. vinegar, for white wine
- 1 tbsp. jalapeño-like fresh spicy chili, or to taste, minced
- 1 tbsp. fresh oregano, chopped or dried
- 4 garlic cloves, or more, sliced, to taste
- Salt and black pepper freshly ground
- 1 (2 to 3 lb. total) whole fish or 2 smaller fish such as striped bass, rockfish, or trout, ideally butter-filled and boned or simply gutted
- 1 lemon sliced
- 4 to 6 sprigs fresh thyme

Directions:

1. Prepare the grill; the heat should be medium-high, and the fire should be about 4 inches from the grate. Combine the tomatoes, 2 tablespoons of olive oil, vinegar, chili, oregano, and a few tablespoons of olive oil.
2. Add the garlic slices and a sprinkle of salt and pepper in a bowl; let sit for 30 minutes at room temperature.
3. Meanwhile, make three or four diagonal, parallel slashes on either side of the fish, just about down to the bone, using a sharp knife. Sprinkle salt and pepper on the inside of the fish, then apply the remaining garlic, a layer of lemon slices, and thyme sprigs. Rub the remaining 2 tablespoons of oil away from the fish and sprinkle with salt and pepper.

4. Grill for 5 to 8 minutes until crisp enough to flip it over. Flip the fish over and cook for 5 to 8 minutes. When the outside is crisp, and a knife moves easily through the meat, the fish is done.

5. Taste the tomato mixture and change the seasoning and if necessary, add more oil. Serve the tomato-toped fish and its liquid.

56. Grilled Redfish with Smoked Tomato Salsa and Black-Eyed Peas

Ingredients:

For the relish of black-eyed pea-jicama:

- 6 tbsp. black-eyed dried peas
- 1 1/2 cups chicken stock or fish
- 2 oz. jicama, peeled and sliced into small 1/4-inch bits
- 1 tbsp. red and yellow bell pepper, each diced
- 1 tbsp. sweet onion, diced
- 1 thin, seeded, and minced serrano chili
- 2 tsp. cucumber diced
- 3 tbsp. mango, papaya, or cantaloupe diced
- 1 tsp. fresh spearmint, finely chopped
- Salt to taste

For the salsa and the smoked tomato:

- 4 (approximately 1 lb.) tomatoes, tiny, very ripe
- 1 tbsp. extra virgin olive oil
- 2 tbsp. orange, red, and yellow bell pepper, each diced
- 3 scallions, including white and green pieces, medium-sized
- 3 small serrano chilies, seeded and diced
- 1/2 cup fresh coriander leaves, minced
- Salt, and freshly ground black pepper to taste
- 4 (6-ounce) redfish fillets
- 2 tbsp. vegetable oil without taste or clarified butter

Directions:

1. 1 hour before serving, make the black-eyed pea relish and soak the black-eyed peas in warm water until they are very soft and slightly larger around 20 to 30 minutes. Bring them to a boil in fish or chicken stock and cook until they are soft but still crisp, about 20 minutes. In a medium-sized bowl, mix peas with the remaining ingredients for relish. With salt, season to taste and blend thoroughly.

2. For the tomato smoking, make a fire in a barbecue with (if possible) briquettes of hardwood. Soak 6 to 8 chunks of aromatic wood or 4 cups of wood chips for 20 minutes in warm water.

3. Add soaked wood chunks when the briquettes are glowing but slightly gray (after about 20 minutes) and let them burn for 5 minutes.

4. Put the tomatoes on your grill. Cover the barbecue and smoke for 10 minutes with the tomatoes, then remove them from the barbecue. Peel tomato, seed, and dice, then set aside.

5. Add enough charcoal to the barbecue to keep the fire hot with plenty of red coal.

6. Heat the olive oil in a large skillet over medium-high heat to make the smoked tomato sauce. Add the peppers, scallions, and serrano chilies and cook for around 3 minutes, until slightly soft. Apply the cilantro and the smoked tomatoes and stir, then season with salt and pepper to taste. Remove the skillet from the heat but keep it warm.

7. Rub fillets on each side with oil to grill the snapper and grill them on the barbecue until they are opaque, and continue to grill for about 4 minutes on each side slightly, not too soft or overly rough. Season with salt and freshly ground pepper.

8. To eat, split the smoked tomato sauce equally between 4 warmed dinner plates. On top of the sauce, put a snapper fillet and spoon relish in a diagonal line over the fillet. Immediately serve.

57. Fillets of White-Fish with Grilled Cabbage

Ingredients:

- Salt
- 4 savoy cabbage leaves
- 8 oz. white-fish fillets, skinless, cut into 4 small pieces like black sea bass, cod, or halibut
- 4 tsp. fresh chopped dill
- salt and black pepper
- Olive oil, as needed
- 1 tbsp. corn) neutral oil, like grapeseed or
- 2 spoonfuls butter
- Multiple fresh thyme sprigs
- 1 Meaty skeleton chopped from a tiny white fish, like a sea bass,
- 2 cups white dry wine
- Microgreens for garnish or flowers

Directions:

1. Heat a rack grill really close to the flame and heat it pretty hot.
2. Bring the water to a boil in a big pot and salt it. Remove the thickest portion of each cabbage leaf's central vein without cutting the leaf in half. Blanch cabbage leaves until just tender (about 30 seconds in boiling water) and then drain on paper towels. Cover with 1 teaspoon of dill, a sprinkle of salt and pepper, and a drizzle of olive oil, and place a slice of fish on one side of each leaf. Fold the other half of the leaf over the fish and trim the edges to create an oval with a large cookie cutter or a knife. Rub it with a little bit of olive oil outside.
3. Put 1 tablespoon of butter and neutral oil in a saucepan large enough to accommodate fish bones in one layer over medium-high heat. Add thyme and fish bones until the butter melts,

and cook, occasionally stirring until very well browned, around 5 minutes. Apply the remaining 1 tablespoon of butter and wine and cook for about 10 minutes, until smooth and reduced in volume. Strain the fish bones and discard them. Season the salt and pepper sauce and hold it over a very low heat when grilling the fish.

4. Grill the fish fillets on each side for 30 seconds—the cabbage should brown and fish should steam, but just barely—you can tell by sticking a toothpick into it if fish is made. It's ready if it encounters a little resistance; if it's really rubbery, it's not. Using an immersion blender or whisk the sauce to foam it up a bit. Sprinkle the sauce with the cabbage and fish, garnish with the microgreens or flowers, and serve.

58. Fish Grilled with Aromatics

Ingredients:

- 4 (1 lb.), saltwater perch, rock cod or snapper or 1 (4-to 5-pound) salmon, heads on
- Vegetable oil used to oil the grill, spatula, and baking dishes
- 6 tbsp. extra virgin olive oil
- 20 garlic cloves with, peeled
- 12 fresh thyme sprigs
- 12 fresh Rosemary sprigs
- 2 bay leaves
- Kosher or coarse sea salt and black pepper, freshly ground, to taste

Directions:

1. Rinse and wipe the fish dry. Only make 3 or 4 shallow cuts through the fish's skin, so that it can expand during cooking. Until ready to cook, refrigerate.
2. Make a fire on an outdoor grill.
3. Preheat the oven to 300°F.
4. Place the grill over the fire and let it heat up for 2 to 3 minutes if the coals are bright red and evenly dusted with ash. Using vegetable oil and paper toweling, thoroughly oil the grill, being careful not to use so much oil that it would spill on coals and cause them to burn up.
5. Place the fish on the grill so that the rungs under it are vertical. Cook until golden grill marks appear on the fish, about 3 minutes on each side. Move fish to one or two oiled baking dishes using a metal spatula lightly brushed with vegetable oil, depending on how many fish you prepare. Place them in the oven and bake for approximately 12 minutes for smaller fish, 20 to 25 minutes for larger fish, or until they are fully opaque.
6. Pour 6 tablespoons of olive oil into an oven-proof dish or ramekin about 10 minutes before the fish is done, then put it in the oven to heat gently. Bring 2 cups of water to a boil over

high heat at the bottom of a steamer. Place the garlic cloves in a steamer, cover and steam for about 8 minutes, or until they are almost tender. In an even layer, add the remaining herbs to the steamer, cover, and continue steaming for 3 minutes.

7. Pour equal amounts of olive oil into the middle of the warmed dinner plates to serve. When preparing small fish, put all of them on top of the oil. Remove the fillets and put the same-sized pieces of fillet on the oil if you are using a big fish such as salmon. Season with coarse salt and pepper to taste. On one side of the plate, arrange the steamed herbs and garlic, and serve immediately.

59. Snapper Grilled with Cumin

Ingredients:

- 4 (9-to 12-ounce) Alaska rose thorn snappers or 2 (1 to 2 lb.) Alaska redfish snappers, cleaned, heads on
- Oil for vegetables
- 1⁄2 tsp. seeds with cumin
- 4 tbsp. plus 2 tsp. Kosher olive oil or raw sea salt to taste.

Directions:

1. Clean the fish and pat it dry. When ready to use, refrigerate.
2. Make an outdoor barbecue fire.
3. Preheat the oven to 300°F.
4. Thoroughly oil grill when coals are bright red and evenly dusted with ash, using vegetable oil and paper toweling.
5. Cut four 1⁄8-inch-deep cuts on either side of each fish when the fire is burning, working a very sharp knife blade under the scales of the fish to make cuts. Push equivalent quantities of cumin seeds firmly into cuts—15 is the optimal amount.
6. With 2 teaspoons of olive oil, rub each fish all over. Place the fish on the grill so the rungs under the body of the fish are vertical. Cook until there are golden grill marks on the fish, no more than 3 minutes on each side for a small fish, 4 to 5 minutes for a big one.
7. Move the fish to an oven-proof dish or baking sheet covered with foil using a lightly oiled metal spatula and continue cooking in the oven until the fish is fully opaque, 8 to 10 minutes for a small fish, 15 to 20 minutes for a larger fish.
8. Stick the tip of a sharp knife into the meat just behind the head of the fish and measure the fish for thickness—the meat has to be visible.

9. Place the remaining 4 tablespoons of olive oil in an oven-proof dish or ramekin about 5 minutes before the fish is done, and place it in the oven to heat gently.

10. Place each fish in the middle of a dinner plate to serve. On one side of the fish, pour 1 tablespoon of warm olive oil, and on the other side of the fish, pour a thin strip of coarse salt. Remove fillets and put equal-sized pieces of fillet on each plate, garnish with salt and oil if you are using larger fish. Immediately serve.

60. The Whole Porgy Grilled with Lime Butter

Ingredients:

- 4 whole porgies, cleaned-up
- 1⁄4 cup olive oil
- 1 large lime
- 10 spoonfuls butter
- 1 tbsp. shallots, finely chopped
- 1 cup white dry vermouth
- 1⁄4 cup fresh lime juice
- 1⁄4 tsp. lime zest, finely grated or chopped
- 1 tbsp. fresh chives, finely chopped

Directions:

1. Preheat a well-scrubbed outdoor gas grill to high, or grill a charcoal grill with fire coals until they are white-hot.
2. Keep a heavy kitchen knife at an angle and score both sides of each porgy, at three equidistant spots, slicing down to the bone.
3. Lightly brush the grill with grease. Brush the fish with oil on both sides and put it on the grill. On top of each fish, squeeze a little lime juice. Grill the fish for around 6 minutes on one each side, or until they can be removed from the grill without sticking—depending on the fish size, the cooking time can vary. Turn and cook for around 6 minutes.
4. Meanwhile, in a pan, heat 1 tablespoon of butter and add the shallots. Cook for about 1 minute, stirring. Add the vermouth, lime juice, and zest and cook until the liquid is almost but not completely evaporated, over high heat.

5. Using a wire whisk to incorporate the remaining 9 tablespoons of butter, stirring quickly. Cook until it's melted and very hot with butter. Withdraw from the sun.

6. On a tray, arrange the fish and pour the hot lime-butter sauce over them. Sprinkle and serve immediately with chives.

61. Grilled Sardines

Ingredients:

- 24 sardines, medium or large, cleaned
- 2 tbsp. extra virgin olive oil
- Salt as well as freshly ground pepper
- A handful of fresh rosemary sprigs with lemon wedges

Directions:

1. To make sure the grill is oiled, prepare a hot grill. Rinse the sardines with paper towels and rinse them. Season with salt and pepper and toss in olive oil.

2. Toss the rosemary sprigs directly into the fire when the grill is ready. Wait for the flames to die down, then if possible, put the sardines directly over heat in batches. Grill on each side for a minute or two, depending on duration. Use tongs or a large metal spatula to move the fish from the grill into a bowl, and serve with lemon wedges.

CPSIA information can be obtained
at www.ICGtesting.com
Printed in the USA
LVHW060533200221
679363LV00008B/350